Short Walks in Northumbria

Guide to 20 local walks

OS Map data

Published by Collins
An imprint of HarperCollins Publishers
Westerhill Road
Bishopbriggs
Glasgow G64 2QT

HarperCollinsPublishers
1st Floor, Watermarque Building, Ringsend Road,
Dublin 4, Ireland

www.harpercollins.co.uk

First edition 2011
Second edition 2015
Reprinted 2017

Mapping on the inner front cover and all
walking planning maps generated from
Collins Bartholomew digital databases

Printed in China by RR Donnelley APS Co. Ltd.

ISBN 978 0 00 810158 9
10 9 8 7

email: collins.reference@harpercollins.co.uk

 Follow us @collins_ref

Contents

Introduction

Weardale

Walking in Northumbria

Northumbria, more than many other walking areas, is distinguished by the sheer diversity of its landscapes. Flat sandy beaches, dramatic sea cliffs, gentle rural vales, hilltop moorland, rocky peaks as well as an abundance of historic sites and wildlife provide the walker with a huge variety of walking possibilities. Excellent walks are found in the greatest concentration in the Pennine and Cheviot Hills and along the Northumbrian coast, but there are many fine footpaths and Rights of Way throughout the entire region.

In addition, there are a number of established long-distance footpaths in Northumbria. The longest of these is the Pennine Way, but shorter routes include the Cleveland Way (in the southeast of the area), the Weardale Way (from Monkwearmouth to Cowshill), the Derwent Walk Country Park (to the west of Newcastle), and the Waskerley Way, Brandon Bishop Auckland Walk, Lanchester Valley Walk and Deerness Valley Walk (a series of footpaths following the old railway lines to the west of Durham).

Visitors to the Cheviot and Pennine hills should bear in mind that navigation amongst the mass of similarly rounded peaks and buttresses can be tricky, even in clear conditions. There is one other hazard for hill walkers which is entirely predictable. From August onwards grouse shooting takes place on the moors so if you are planning to explore one of the hill routes, check with the local estate or tourist office before doing so.

Walking is a pastime which can fulfil the needs of everyone. You can adapt it to suit your own preferences and it is one of the healthiest of activities. This guide is for those who just want to walk a few miles. It really doesn't take long to find yourself in some lovely countryside. All the walks are five miles or less so should easily be completed in under three hours. Walking can be anything from an individual pastime to a family stroll, or maybe a group of friends enjoying the fresh air and open spaces of our countryside. There is no need for walking to be competitive and, to get the most from a walk, it shouldn't be regarded simply as a means of covering a given distance in the shortest possible time.

What is Northumbria?

Those with an interest in Anglo-Saxon history may consider the title of this book a little misleading. The ancient kingdom of Northumbria assumed many shapes and sizes during its 350 year existence (between AD 604, when it was created by Ethelfrid, and AD 954, when King Edred incorporated it into England), but its core is generally defined as lying between the Rivers Forth and Humber. The 'Northumbria' shown here, and used as the geographical basis for this book, is contained within the regional boundaries of Northumberland, Durham, Cleveland and Tyne and Wear - that is, the old (pre-1974) counties of Northumberland and Durham, plus a little of the North Riding of Yorkshire.

The word 'Northumbria' instantly conjures up a number of iconic images: Durham Cathedral, Geordie coal miners, Holy Island and the intricate tracery of the Lindisfarne Gospels, the bare slopes of the Cheviots, a gaunt peel tower and Hadrian's Wall. In a way, this list provides a key to the major historic periods in the area. The wall is evidence of the time of the Romans, who annexed all of this area at one time or another, while Holy Island reflects the Anglo-Saxon Northumbrians who followed them, and the island's priory and renowned illuminated manuscripts represent the Celtic people who predated both invasions, and who returned to the island bringing the Christian religion with them - only to be evicted by the Vikings. Durham Cathedral is also a symbol of Christianity - it is the burial place of St Cuthbert, the patron saint of Northumbria - but in addition demonstrates the power of the Prince Bishops: a virtually autonomous power in the north, they existed as a buffer between southern England and the Scots. The peel (or pele) tower characterises the three centuries of continuous warfare fought along the line of the Scottish Border, while the bare Cheviots portray the desolation in which these struggles occurred. And, lastly, the miner embodies the coal-mining industry, which underpinned the industrial strength of the North East during the 19th century.

Teesdale

Geology

The underlying geology of Northumbria is sedimentary of carboniferous age rocks with widespread intrusions of igneous rocks such as the Whin Sill. This rugged series of east–west ridges were exploited by the Romans who began building the 72 mile (117km) long Hadrian's Wall in AD 122. Another igneous outcrop is that of The Cheviots which were formed by volcanic action. At their heart is the granite mass of The Cheviot 2674ft (815m). This is surrounded by an area of old red sandstone, between the River Till and Redesdale; while the lower hills at the southern end of the range are composed of carboniferous limestone.

The Pennines are a low-rising mountain range often described as the 'backbone of England' and consist of a carboniferous limestone overlain with millstone grit. This limestone is exposed at the surface in the north of the chain but the general character of the range is that of moorland indented by more fertile river valleys. The Cleveland Hills are also topped by moorland but are formed by soft Lower Jurassic rocks interspersed with hard Middle Jurassic sandstone creating features such as the landmark peak of Roseberry Topping.

Wildlife in Northumbria

There is a wide variety of natural habitats in Northumbria, ranging from the damp moorland of the Cheviots and Pennines, through the sheltered dales and eastern farmland, to the raw North Sea coast, with its mud flats and sand dunes. Within this area are two large Nature Reserves - the mud flats and dunes of Lindisfarne and the open moorland of Upper Teesdale. The area is divided into a number of separate environments - Commercial Forestry, Woodland, Hills and Moorland, Farmland, Freshwater, and Seashore.

There was little coniferous woodland in Northumbria until commercial forestry began in the 1920s. A number of large forests are found throughout the area, and one positively huge one at Kielder, on the southern hills of the Cheviots. These plantations provide cover for rabbit, fox, red and grey squirrel and roe deer. The trees planted are quite varied and can include Scots and lodge-pole pine, Sitka and Norway spruce, Japanese and European larch, Douglas fir and others. Within these habitats it may be possible to spot crossbill, siskin, goldcrest, coal tit, redpoll and long-eared owl.

The original forest of broad-leaved trees which once covered much of Northumbria has now virtually disappeared, although small patches can be found along some of the routes in the book.

Woodland can provide the richest of inland habitats. Common species of trees throughout Northumbria include oak, hazel, beech, yew, ash, hawthorn and sycamore, with alder, sallow and willow in riverside woods. These provide a breeding ground for insects (the oak being particularly rich in this respect) which in turn attract birds such as pied and spotted flycatchers, green and great spotted woodpeckers, treecreeper, willow warbler and blackcap. Other woodland species include the wren, blackbird, song thrush, blue tit and great tit, plus birds of prey, such as the sparrowhawk and tawny owl.

Woodland mammals include small mice, voles and shrews, and the larger fox, badger, hedgehog, red and grey squirrel, roe deer, weasel and stoat. On the woodland floor, common wild flower species include foxglove, primrose, wood sorrel, lesser celandine, wood anemone, violet and bluebell.

The rounded hills of the Cheviots and the Pennines are covered in large swathes of grass and heather moorland. Each spring, areas of heather will be burnt from the moors to encourage new growth, which, in turn, attracts red grouse. This bird can be met on virtually any high-level walk, and is usually seen springing up from the heather with a loud, chuckling cry.

A rarer resident of the high ground is the peregrine falcon: a masterful flyer which takes its prey on the wing. Other birds of prey include the merlin and the hen harrier, while the short-eared owl can sometimes be seen hawking over the moors. Other birds to be found on the moors include the blackcock, snipe, curlew, lapwing, carrion crow and wheatear.

On heather moors the customary cover is ling heather, while damp areas of moor support bog cotton, bog asphodel, bog mosses and cranberry. In Upper Teesdale, however, the cover is sufficiently different to have warranted the establishment of a Nature Reserve where some plant species such as the spring gentian, Teesdale violet and alpine forget-me-not have been present since the end of the last Ice Age.

Farmland extends over a huge proportion of Northumbria. On the flat, coastal areas the land is almost entirely arable, while on the inland hills it is a mixture of arable and grazing. With all this variety, it is difficult to generalise about species. However, plants which may be found throughout the farmland include coltsfoot, dandelion, scabious, birdsfoot trefoil, cowslip, bugle and tufted vetch.

Many of the lower fields are lined with hedges, which encourage finches, sparrows, robin, linnet, wren, blackbird, thrushes and others, while larger birds include magpie, lapwing, curlew, snipe, pheasant and partridge plus redwing, fieldfare and waxwing in the winter months. Of birds of prey, the one most seen over farmland is the kestrel.

In Northumbria there is one semi-domesticated species worthy of note: the wild white cattle of Chillingham Castle (southeast of Wooler). This small herd is considered to be the purest remnant of the cattle of Bronze Age England. Walk 4 is a circuit of Chillingham Park.

The freshwater habitat is rather broad, covering everything from upland bogs to wide rivers and lakes. In the upper waters, the most common birds are the dipper and the grey and pied wagtails, which feed off insect larvae in the streams, as do tiny trout which can readily be seen in the larger pools. Often these waters will flow through narrow, wooded valleys. In such places, the kingfisher may be glimpsed, while more open water may attract heron, coot, moorhen, dabchick, great crested grebe and a variety of duck species. There are few mammals which specifically live by the water, but both the otter and the mink are present in this area.

Any naturalist reflecting on the Northumbrian coast brings to mind immediately the Fame Islands: a small archipelago offshore from Bamburgh. These small, rocky islands are incredibly rich in breeding seabirds - including puffin, guillemot, kittiwake, fulmar, razorbill, cormorant, shag and eider duck - while also having a colony of grey seals.

There is a small area of tidal mud at the mouth of the River Tees, and a larger one around Holy Island and Budle Bay, incorporated into what is now the Lindisfarne National Nature Reserve. The mud flats are of particular interest for the large numbers of wildfowl and waders. Wildfowl to be seen during the winter months include mallard, teal, wigeon and pintail, greylag and pale-bellied brent. While, of waders, there are greenshank, redshank, curlew, whimbrel, sanderling, little stint, bar-tailed godwit, dunlin, knot, oystercatcher and turnstone.

As well as mud flats, the Nature Reserve includes large areas of sand dunes, both on the island and on the mainland. These moving masses of loose sand are bound together by marram grass, while other plants to be found in this dry environment include hound's tongue, viper's bugloss and bloody cranesbill. Holy Island also has breeding colonies of little and sandwich terns.

Northumbria National Parks

Walkers can enjoy the scenic wilderness of two contrasting National Parks found in Northumbria. The Northumberland National Park was designated in 1956 and stretches from Hadrian's Wall in the south to the Cheviot Hills and Scottish border in the north covering a total of 405 square miles (1,049 sq km). From Iron Age hillforts to the legacy of the Romans and remnants of the Victorian industrial age, the sites of interest are numerous. Three informative National Park Centres are situated in Rothbury, Ingram and Once Brewed near Hadrian's Wall. 'The Wall' can be seen at many locations but 28 miles (46km) of the best preserved sections lie within the Northumberland National Park and include the World Heritage Site at Housesteads.

The northern edge of the North York Moors National Park is also featured in this book. Designated a National Park in 1952, this is one of the largest expanses of heather moorland in the United Kingdom and covers a total of 554 square miles (1,434 sq km). The spectacular scenery where the Cleveland Hills meet the North Sea has been declared Heritage Coast and the Boulby cliffs rising to 690ft (210m) are

Old alum quarries

the highest point on the east coast of England. This popular recreational expanse of countryside includes the Cleveland Way, a long distance walk encircling the moorland plateau with far reaching, wide-open views.

Walking tips & guidance

Safety

As with all other outdoor activities, walking is safe provided a few simple commonsense rules are followed:

- Make sure you are fit enough to complete the walk;
- Always try to let others know where you intend going, especially if you are walking alone;
- Be clothed adequately for the weather and always wear suitable footwear;
- Always allow plenty of time for the walk, especially if it is longer or harder than you have done before;
- Whatever the distance you plan to walk, always allow plenty of daylight hours unless you are absolutely certain of the route;
- If mist or bad weather come on unexpectedly, do not panic but instead try to remember the last certain feature which you have passed (road, farm, wood, etc.). Then work out your route from that point on the map but be sure of your route before continuing;
- Do not dislodge stones on the high edges: there may be climbers or other walkers on the lower crags and slopes;

- Unfortunately, accidents can happen even on the easiest of walks. If this should be the case and you need the help of others, make sure that the injured person is safe in a place where no further injury is likely to occur. For example, the injured person should not be left on a steep hillside or in danger from falling rocks. If you have a mobile phone and there is a signal, call for assistance. If, however, you are unable to contact help by mobile and you cannot leave anyone with the injured person, and even if they are conscious, try to leave a written note explaining their injuries and whatever you have done in the way of first aid treatment. Make sure you know exactly where you left them and then go to find assistance. Make your way to a telephone, dial 999 and ask for the police or mountain rescue. Unless the accident has happened within easy access of a road, it is the responsibility of the police to arrange evacuation. Always give accurate directions on how to find the casualty and, if possible, give an indication of the injuries involved;

- When walking in open country, learn to keep an eye on the immediate foreground while you admire the scenery or plan the route ahead. This may sound difficult but will enhance your walking experience;

- It's best to walk at a steady pace, always on the flat of the feet as this is less tiring. Try not to walk directly up or downhill. A zigzag route is a more comfortable way of negotiating a slope. Running directly downhill is a major cause of erosion on popular hillsides;

- When walking along a country road, walk on the right, facing the traffic. The exception to this rule is, when approaching a blind bend, the walker should cross over to the left and so have a clear view and also be seen in both directions;

- Finally, always park your car where it will not cause inconvenience to other road users or prevent a farmer from gaining access to his fields. Take any valuables with you or lock them out of sight in the car.

Equipment

Equipment, including clothing, footwear and rucksacks, is essentially a personal thing and depends on several factors, such as the type of activity planned, the time of year, and weather likely to be encountered.

All too often, a novice walker will spend money on a fashionable jacket but will skimp when it comes to buying footwear or a comfortable rucksack. Blistered and tired feet quickly remove all enjoyment from even the most exciting walk and a poorly balanced rucksack will soon feel as though you are carrying a ton of bricks. Well designed equipment is not only more comfortable but, being better made, it is longer lasting.

Clothing should be adequate for the day. In summer, remember to protect your head and neck, which are particularly vulnerable in a strong sun and use sun screen. Wear light woollen socks and lightweight boots or strong shoes. A spare pullover and waterproofs carried in the rucksack should, however, always be there in case you need them.

Winter wear is a much more serious affair. Remember that once the body starts to lose heat, it becomes much less efficient. Jeans are particularly unsuitable for winter wear and can sometimes even be downright dangerous.

Waterproof clothing is an area where it pays to buy the best you can afford. Make sure that the jacket is loose-fitting, windproof and has a generous hood. Waterproof overtrousers will not only offer complete protection in the rain but they are also windproof. Do not be misled by flimsy nylon 'showerproof' items. Remember, too, that garments made from rubberised or plastic material are heavy to carry and wear and they trap body condensation. Your rucksack should have wide, padded carrying straps for comfort.

It is important to wear boots that fit well or shoes with a good moulded sole – blisters can ruin any walk! Woollen socks are much more comfortable than any other fibre. Your clothes should be comfortable and not likely to catch on twigs and bushes.

It is important to carry a compass, preferably one of the 'Silva' type as well as this guide. A smaller scale map covering a wider area can add to the enjoyment of a walk. Binoculars are not essential but are very useful for spotting distant stiles and give added interest to viewpoints and wildlife. Although none of the walks in this guide venture too far from civilisation, on a hot day even the shortest of walks can lead to dehydration so a bottle of water is advisable.

Finally, a small first aid kit is an invaluable help in coping with cuts and other small injuries.

Public Rights of Way

In 1949, the National Parks and Access to the Countryside Act tidied up the law covering rights of way. Following public consultation, maps were drawn up by the Countryside Authorities of England and Wales to show all the rights of way. Copies of these maps are available for public inspection and are invaluable when trying to resolve doubts over little-used footpaths. Once on the map, the right of way is irrefutable.

Right of way means that anyone may walk freely on a defined footpath or ride a horse or pedal cycle along a public bridleway. No one may interfere with this right and the walker is within his rights if he removes any obstruction along the route, provided that he has not set out purposely with the intention of removing that obstruction. All obstructions should be reported to the local Highways Authority.

In England and Wales rights of way fall into three main categories:

- Public Footpaths – for walkers only;
- Bridleways – for passage on foot, horseback, or bicycle;
- Byways – for all the above and for motorized vehicles

Free access to footpaths and bridleways does mean that certain guidelines should be followed as a courtesy to those who live and work in the area. For example, you should only sit down to picnic where it does not interfere with other walkers or the landowner. All gates must be kept closed to prevent stock from straying and dogs must be kept under close control – usually this is interpreted as meaning that they should be kept on a leash. Motor vehicles must not be driven along a public footpath or bridleway without the landowner's consent.

A farmer can put a docile mature beef bull with a herd of cows or heifers, in a field crossed by a public footpath. Beef bulls such as Herefords (usually brown/red colour) are unlikely to be upset by passers by but dairy bulls, like the black and white Friesian, can be dangerous by nature. It is, therefore, illegal for a farmer to let a dairy bull roam loose in a field open to public access.

The Countryside and Rights of Way Act 2000 (the 'right to roam') allows access on foot to areas of legally defined 'open country' – mountain, moor, downland, heath and registered common land. You will find these areas shaded orange on the maps in this guide. It does not allow freedom to walk anywhere. It also increases protection for Sites of Special Scientific Interest, improves wildlife enforcement legislation and allows better management of Areas of Outstanding Natural Beauty.

Route marker

The Country Code

The Country Code has been designed not as a set of hard and fast rules, although they do have the backing of the law, but as a statement of commonsense. The code is a gentle reminder of how to behave in the countryside. Walkers should walk with the intention of leaving the place exactly as it was before they arrived. There is a saying that a good walker 'leaves only footprints and takes only photographs', which really sums up the code perfectly.

Never walk more than two abreast on a footpath as you will erode more ground by causing an unnatural widening of paths. Also try to avoid the spread of trodden ground around a boggy area. Mud soon cleans off boots but plant life is slow to grow back once it has been worn away.

Have respect for everything in the countryside, be it those beautiful flowers found along the way or a farmer's gate which is difficult to close.

Stone walls were built at a time when labour costs were a fraction of those today and the special skills required to build or repair them have almost disappeared. Never climb over or onto stone walls; always use stiles and gates.

Dogs which chase sheep can cause them to lose their lambs and a farmer is within his rights if he shoots a dog which he believes is worrying his stock.

The moors and woodlands are often tinder dry in summer, so take care not to start a fire. A fire caused by something as simple as a discarded cigarette can burn for weeks, once it gets deep down into the underlying peat.

When walking across fields or enclosed land, make sure that you read the map carefully and avoid trespassing. As a rule, the line of a footpath or right of way, even when it is not clearly defined on the ground, can usually be followed by lining up stiles or gates.

Obviously flowers and plants encountered on a walk should not be taken but left for others passing to enjoy. To use the excuse 'I have only taken a few' is futile. If everyone only took a few the countryside would be devastated. If young wild animals are encountered they should be left well alone. For instance, if a fawn or a deer calf is discovered lying still in the grass it would be wrong to assume that it has been abandoned. Mothers hide their offspring while they go away to graze and browse and return to them at feeding time. If the animals are touched it could mean that they will be abandoned as the human scent might deter the mother from returning to her offspring. Similarly with baby birds, who have not yet mastered flight; they may appear to have been abandoned but often are being watched by their parents who might be waiting for a walker to pass on before coming out to give flight lesson two!

What appear to be harmful snakes should not be killed because firstly the 'snake' could be a slow worm, which looks like a snake but is really a harmless legless lizard, and second, even if it were an adder (they are quite common) it will escape if given the opportunity. Adders are part of the pattern of nature and should not be persecuted. They rarely bite unless they are handled; a foolish act, which is not uncommon; or trodden on, which is rare, as the snakes are usually basking in full view and are very quick to escape.

Map reading

Some people find map reading so easy that they can open a map and immediately relate it to the area of countryside in which they are standing. To others, a map is as unintelligible as ancient Greek! A map is an accurate but flat picture of the three-dimensional features of the countryside. Features such as roads, streams, woodland and buildings are relatively easy to identify, either from their shape or position. Heights, on the other hand, can be difficult to interpret from the single dimension of a map. The Ordnance Survey 1:25,000 mapping used in this guide shows the contours at 5 metre intervals. Summits and spot heights are also shown.

The best way to estimate the angle of a slope, as shown on any map, is to remember that if the contour lines come close together then the slope is steep – the closer together the contours the steeper the slope.

Learn the symbols for features shown on the map and, when starting out on a walk, line up the map with one or more features, which are recognisable both from the map and on the ground. In this way, the map will be correctly positioned relative to the terrain. It should then only be necessary to look from the map towards the footpath or objective of your walk and then make for it! This process is also useful for determining your position at any time during the walk.

Let's take the skill of map reading one stage further: sometimes there are no easily recognisable features nearby: there may be the odd clump of trees and a building or two but none of them can be related exactly to the map. This is a frequent occurrence but there is a simple answer to the problem and this is where the use of a compass comes in. Simply place the map on the ground, or other flat surface, with the compass held gently above the map. Turn the map until the edge is parallel to the line of the compass needle, which should point to the top of the map. Lay the compass on the map and adjust the position of both, making sure that the compass needle still points to the top of the map and is parallel to the edge. By this method, the map is orientated in a north-south alignment. To find your position on the map, look out for prominent features and draw imaginary lines from them down on to the map. Your position is where these lines cross. This method of map reading takes a little practice before you can become proficient but it is worth the effort.

How to use this book

This book contains route maps and descriptions for 20 walks, with areas of interest indicated by symbols (see below). For each walk particular points of interest are denoted by a number both in the text and on the map (where the number appears in a circle). In the text the route instructions are prefixed by a capital letter. We recommend that you read the whole description, including the fact box at the start of each walk, before setting out.

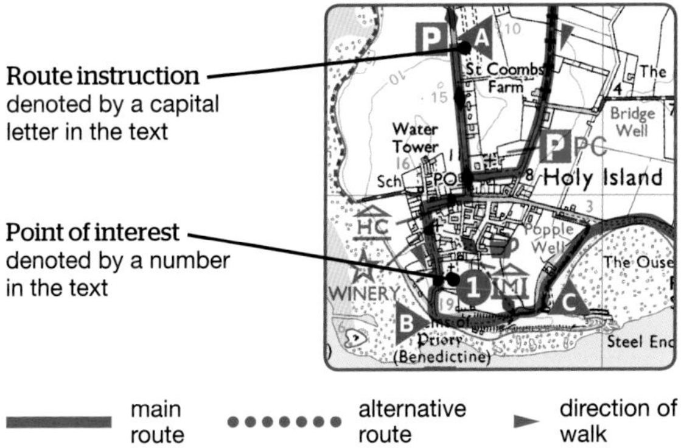

Key to walk symbols

At the start of each walk there is a series of symbols that indicate particular areas of interest associated with the route.

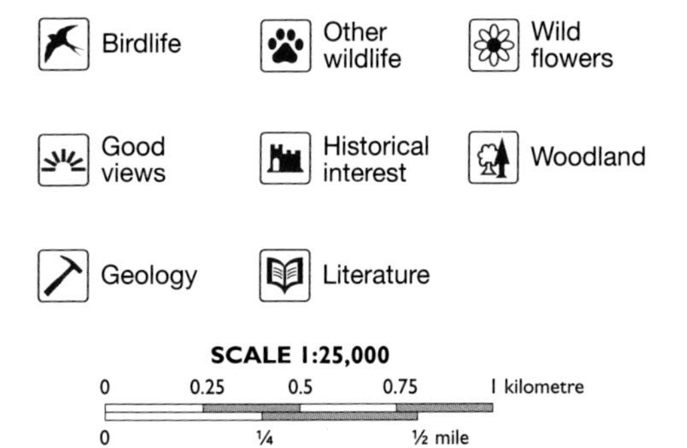

Please note the scale for walk maps is 1:25,000 unless otherwise stated
North is always at the top of the page

“A pleasant short walk along a rough path beside the lovely River Tweed. Walk to Scotland across the Ladykirk and Norham Bridge and admire the views up and downstream”

Norham is a small village by the River Tweed, chiefly famous for its fine 12th century castle, built by the Bishop of Durham. Also of significance is the Ladykirk and Norham bridge, opened in 1864 to replace an earlier wooden structure connecting England to Scotland. Even before the wooden bridge, there was a great ford providing a place to cross the river. St Aidan crossed the border here on his way from Iona to Lindisfarne (see walk 2) in AD635 and for centuries after, it became one of the most important crossings on the Tweed. It was here that Edward I of England met the Scots nobility in 1292 to decide on the future king of Scotland.

Norham

View south from the bridge over the River Tweed

Plan your walk

DISTANCE: 2 miles (3km)

TIME: 1 hour

START/END: NT899473 Norham village green

TERRAIN: Easy

MAPS:
OS Explorer 339;
OS Landranger 74

Route instructions

1 Norham Castle: now a stately ruin on a mound above the river at the eastern end of the village – was one of the major English strongholds along the Border, and witnessed a great deal of fighting during the centuries of Anglo-Scottish warfare.

A For this walk, park in the centre of Norham 8 miles (13km) southwest of Berwick on the A698/B6470, and take the track from the village green, passing to the right of the graveyard, down to the river.

B Once at the river turn left, along what starts as a wide, clear track. The border runs along the centre of the river at this point, so the steep bank on the far side of the water is in Scotland. When the track ends, continue along a rough path. When there is minimum foliage, there are fine views looking back to the castle while, to the left the parish church is visible across the farmland.

C Continue along the riverbank until the bridge is reached. Either climb up the steps and cross the road, or else follow the path under the four-span bridge and then cut left, over a stile, to rejoin the correct path; running beside a fence to the right of a field above the river.

D Near the end of the field there is a stile over the fence

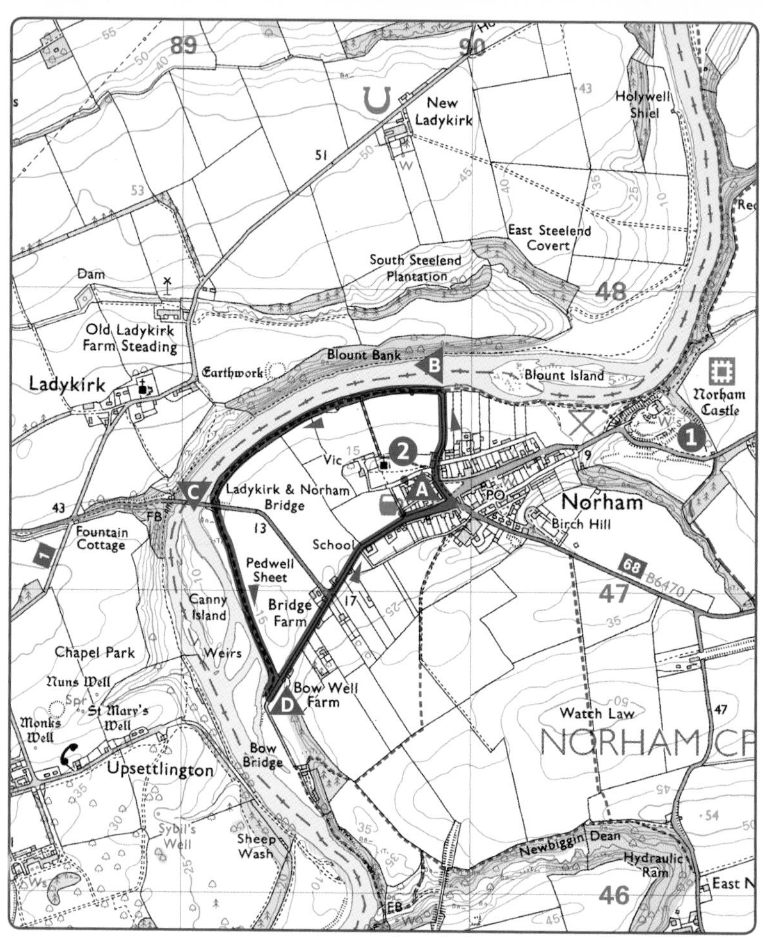

to the right. Cross this and then continue to a gate onto the road. Turn left to return to Norham. There are additional footpaths by the river: westwards (turn right at the road) to Twizel Bridge, and eastwards (from beyond the castle) to Horncliffe and beyond.

2 To visit St Cuthberts parish church turn left as you return to the village. In 1320 the church was occupied and fortified by Robert the Bruce during a siege of the castle and it is likely that an earlier 9th century church once stood beneath the current site. Parts of the original Norman church remain, but considerable rebuilding was undertaken in the 17th and 19th centuries.

Norham

St Cuthberts Church

“A wonderfully varied circuit on a tidal island steeped in history taking in a pretty village, a ruined priory, a wide harbour, a landmark castle, sand dunes and sweeping coastal scenery”

Holy Island, or Lindisfarne, is a small, square island; little more than a mile (1.6km) square, with one long, sandy promontory, the Snook, reaching out westwards towards the mainland. It is only an island for around half of each day; the rest of the time it is joined to the mainland by a road across a mile (1.5km) long causeway over the wide sands and mud-flats which are now incorporated into the Lindisfarne National Nature Reserve. It is a place of unique beauty, and of enormous historical importance. Indeed, it holds a place in English religious history which parallels the importance of Iona in Scotland.

Holy Island

Fishing boat shed and Priory ruins

Plan your walk

DISTANCE: 3½ miles (5.5km)

TIME: 1¾ hours

START/END: NU127420 Holy Island main car park

It is essential to check the local tide tables (check at tourist information centres or www.northumberlandlife.org/holy-island/) before planning a trip to the island

TERRAIN: Easy

MAPS:
OS Explorer 340;
OS Landranger 75

Route instructions

A Turn left out of the car park. Go straight on at the first junction, right at the t-junction, and walk on down the main street. Turn left at the end of the street and walk on down a street, then along a lane beyond, which passes St Mary's church and continues down to the shore.

B Turn left, along the shore, then climb up on to a low ridge along the southern edge of the island. From this point there are fine views in all directions. Continue along the ridge until it drops down towards the harbour.

1 From this ridge there are good views looking down on Lindisfarne Priory ruins which was once one of the most important centres of early Christianity in Anglo-Saxon England and it still remains a site of pilgrimage today. There is a museum on the edge of the village detailing the history and development of the priory.

C Join the track which runs along the head of the little bay, past the row of upturned fishing boats which are now used as sheds. On the north edge of the bay, the track joins a road leading out towards the castle – now owned by the National Trust and open to the public.

2 The castle is perched on a rocky ridge and is a

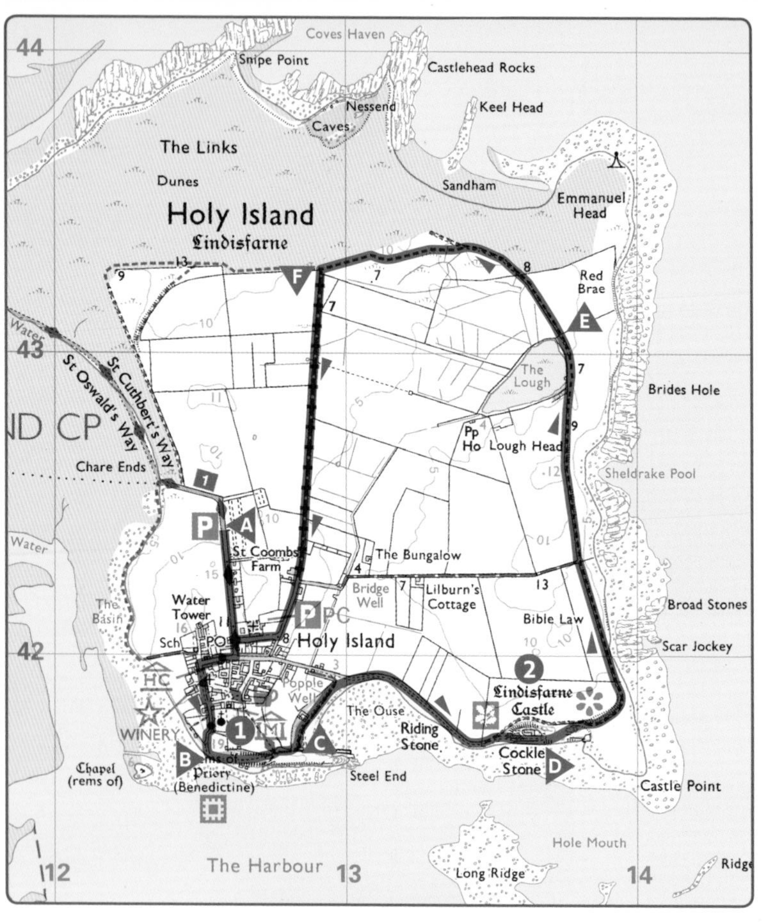

landmark visible from many miles of the Northumbrian coastline. It was originally a Tudor fort which was then converted into a private house in 1903.

D Walk beyond the castle, past the old lime kilns, and join the track which curves to the left, inland from Castle Point, to shadow the eastern edge of the island. Follow this track past a small lake.

E There is a stile across the track near the end of the lake. A short distance beyond, there is a kissing gate. Proceed through this and then, after about 100yds (90m), cut left along a grassy track. Immediately there is a fork in this track: take the right-hand route. Continue along this path, which runs along the edge of the sand dunes on the northern edge of the island.

Holy Island

F When the track reaches a junction, turn left through a gate and follow a straight track back into the village. Turn right before the no entry signs to return to the car park.

It was from Iona that the earliest Celtic missionaries came to the island. King Oswald of Northumbria, during a period of misfortune, spent a number of years in exile in Scotland, during which time he was converted to Christianity. When he had re-established himself at Bamburgh (see walk 3) (a short distance to the south, along the coast), he sent to Iona for a missionary. In 635 St Aidan arrived and established a mission on Holy Island, within sight of his patron's castle.

The mission was spectacularly successful, and remained a centre of religion and learning until, in June 793, the Vikings arrived. In this and subsequent raids the Christian centres in Northumberland were effectively destroyed. An attempt was made to rebuild the church on Holy Island, but by 875 the situation had become impossible and the island was deserted.

Following the period of Viking rule the island was reinhabited by a cell of Benedictine monks, at the end of the 11th century. It was they who built the priory – dedicated to the most famous Bishop of Lindisfarne, St Cuthbert. The building survived the ravages of the Border wars, before falling during the dissolution of the monasteries, in 1541, at which time much of the stone was removed for use in the construction of the castle – intended as a further defence against the Scots.

The Lough and dunes on Holy Island

> “A scenic coastal walk passing one of the largest inhabited castles in the country whilst enjoying far reaching views to the Farne Islands”

As well as its great castle Bamburgh enjoys a varied coastline of sweeping beaches, dunes and rocky shores. A few miles north of Bamburgh is Budel Bay, a vast expanse of mud flats, home to thousands of sea and land birds. This bay was an important port in the 13th century but the harbour has long since disappeared beneath the sands and silt. The tidal sands now provide a home to wintering wildfowl and wading birds. Species such as greylag and pink-footed geese, mallard, and wigeon migrate here in late summer from the Arctic to spend the winter months in this southern corner of the Lindisfarne National Nature Reserve.

Bamburgh

Harkess Rocks

Route instructions

1 The impressive structure of Bamburgh Castle dominates this village: a great mass of red sandstone on an abrupt dolerite rock above the North Sea. The rock has been used as a stronghold from at least Anglo-Saxon times, but the oldest section of the building still in use is the great keep, dating from the 12th century. Additions and repairs to the structure were still being made at the turn of the century. The castle is open to the public for part of the year.

A Starting from the centre of Bamburgh, walk north on a street called 'The Wynding' to the edge of the village and then cut down to the sandy shore. If the tide is in, it may be necessary to follow the road, and the path beyond, a little inland from the coast; but otherwise it is best to walk along the shore, across the sands and over the Harkess Rocks. Continue beyond, round the point to Budle Bay – a large tidal inlet of mud and sand, of particular interest for its sand dunes, and for the large numbers of wildfowl and waders which it attracts.

B Either return by the same route or skirt the caravan park to Kiln point. If the tide is out, bear right at the caravan park and walk this stretch along the beach before turning left up a track to the road. Otherwise follow the left

Plan your walk

DISTANCE: 5 miles (8km)

TIME: 2½ hours

START/END: NU180349 Bamburgh

TERRAIN: Easy

MAPS:
OS Explorer 340;
OS Landranger 75

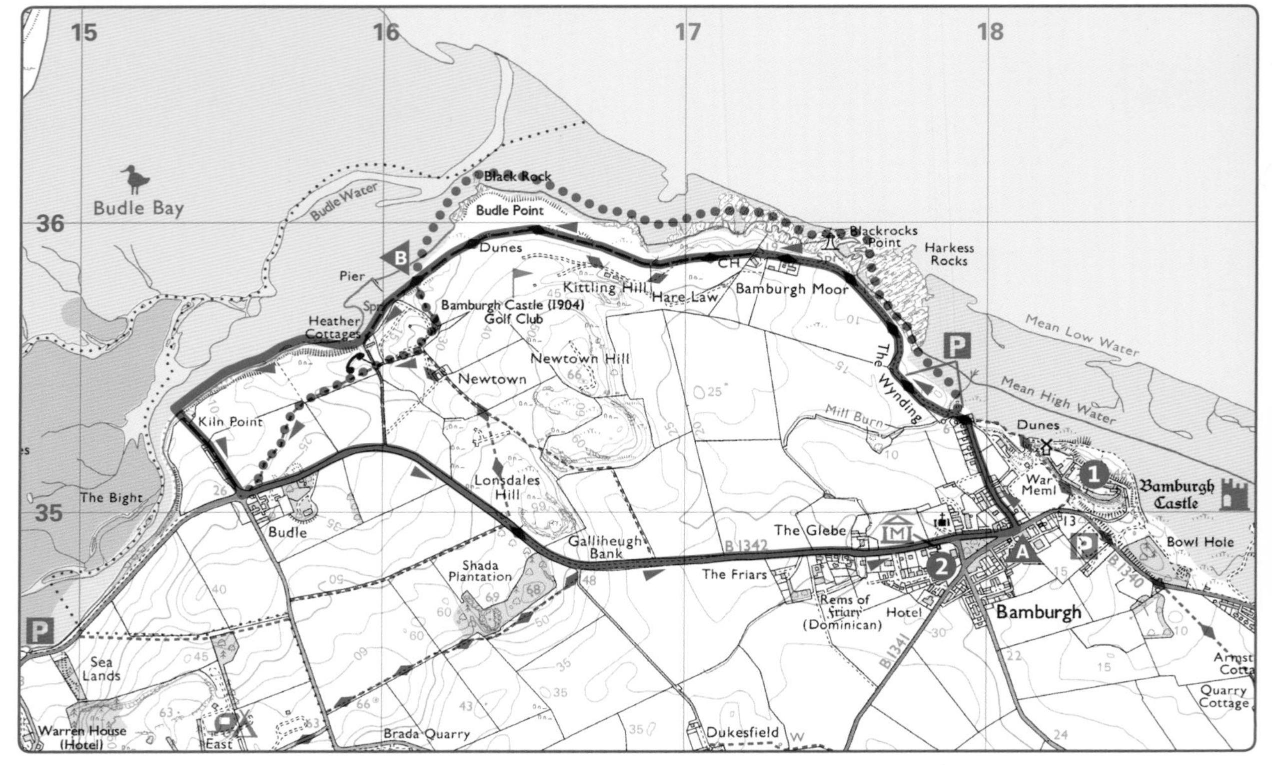
Budle Bay
Budle Water
Black Rock
Budle Point
Dunes
Pier
Heather Cottages
Kiln Point
The Bight
Budle
Bamburgh Castle (1904) Golf Club
Kittling Hill
Hare Law
Bamburgh Moor
Blackrocks Point
Harkess Rocks
Newtown Hill
Newtown
Lonsdales Hill
Galliheugh Bank
Shada Plantation
The Wynding
Mill Burn
Mean Low Water
Mean High Water
Dunes
War Meml
Bamburgh Castle
Bowl Hole
The Glebe
The Friars
Rems of friary (Dominican)
Hotel
Bamburgh
B1342
B1341
B1340
Sea Lands
Warren House (Hotel)
East
Brada Quarry
Dukesfield
Quarry Cottage
15
16
17
18
35
36

Bamburgh

path above the caravan site and across fields to the road. The B1342 back to Bamburgh is a pleasant enough walk, but it can be busy during the summer, and should then be avoided.

2 Another attraction of Bamburgh is the charming Grace Darling Museum. The centrepiece of the collection is the coble (the traditional fishing boat of the North East) in which Grace and her father rescued the crew of the SS Forfarshire in 1838. Opposite the museum is St Aidan's Church containing a window depicting the heroics of Grace Darling and the churchyard is home to the ornate Grace Darling Memorial.

Grace Darling Memorial

“A circuit of Chillingham Park, climbing through woodland to a ridge with impressive rural views”

The Chillingham Wild Cattle have been grazing in Chillingham Park for over 700 years, and are now managed by a charitable trust which also owns the park. Their genetic isolation make them rare survivors of the beasts which would have roamed the forests of medieval England. They are untamed and unpredictable so don't enter their enclosure other than on a tour with a warden. Nearby Chillingham Castle is well worth a visit.

Chillingham Wild Cattle

walk 4

Chillingham Cattle

Plan your walk

DISTANCE: 4½ miles (7.25km)

TIME: 2½ hours

START/END: NU073257 Chillingham Park

TERRAIN: Moderate

MAPS: OS Explorer 340; OS Landranger 75

Route instructions

A Park on the road beyond the church and walk up to a gate 165 yards (150m) beyond the top car park (which is for paying tour visitors only). Follow signed route through gate, diagonally across field and through another gate to the Hemmel meeting point, where cattle tours start.

1 The Hemmel is a fine open-fronted stone cowshed, and has a small exhibition relating to the cattle and park.

B Follow sign to 'Forest Walk' through trees, to a gate and then up a wide path between two fields. After ¼ mile (400m) turn right. Go through two gates and up a slope to a kissing gate and a gravelled track.

C Turn right onto the track, then almost immediately left, along a sunken grass track. Climb up past a viewpoint and picnic tables to a gate. Continue on, downhill through the woods to a stile to the left of a gate.

2 There are only 100 wild cattle, but numbers went as low as 13 after a fierce winter in 1947. They seem to survive despite their inbreeding.

D Cross the gravel track, go around a gate and follow the path with a plantation on your left. When the path splits, bear left, signposted 'Forest Walk'. Climb up

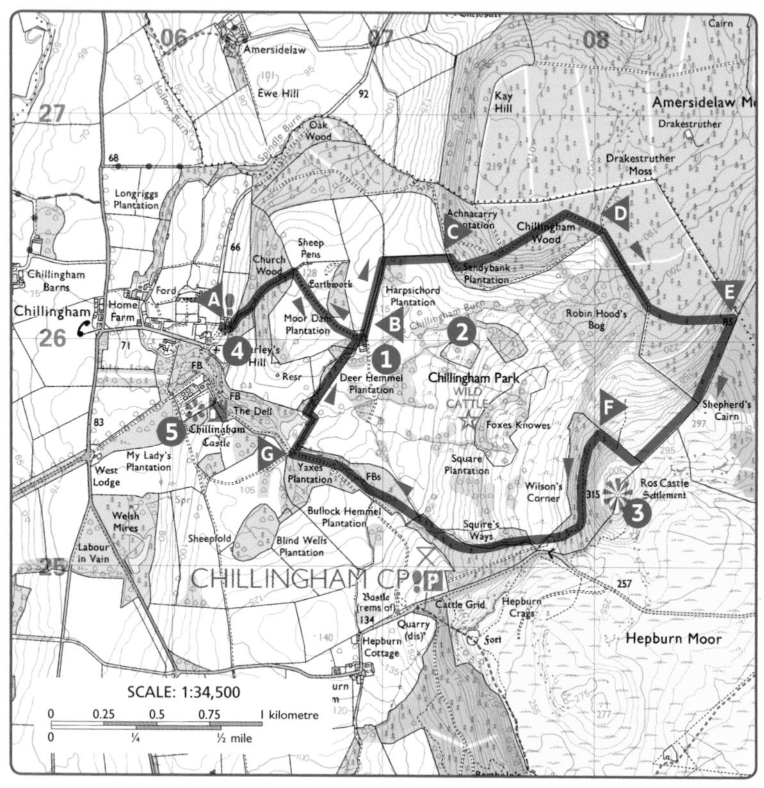

through a plantation as far as a gate in a long wall.

E Turn right to follow a path with the wall on your left. Eventually you emerge onto moorland with panoramic views over the park. Follow the ridge until the fence turns downhill. Turn right and follow the path to where there is a gate on the right.

3 Ros Castle is a 3000 year-old hill fort atop Ros Hill. It is 1034ft (315m) high and offers good views, but access from this route is tricky.

F Follow the sign left to Hepburn. The path snakes gradually downhill. Where it splits, bear right away from the wall rather than towards the gate ahead. Continue on down and over a gulley at the point where it meets a stream. Ignore a gate to your left as the path meanders on, over a small stone bridge and then through a gap in a wall. Look out for arrow signs made using sheep bones. Path then winds through large pines, over a bridge and on through more woods.

Chillingham Wild Cattle

G On reaching a wide track, turn right and walk with a fence on your left, past a pond. At a gate, dog-leg left and continue with a fence on your right. This leads over a stream and back up to the Hemmel. From here you can retrace your steps across the field to the car park.

4 St Peter's Church is a modest medieval building with Victorian box pews. Sir Ralph Grey's magnificent and serene tomb belies his brutality. He condemned his own son to death for supporting the other side in the Wars of the Roses.

5 Chillingham Castle is an impressive fortress dating from the 12th century. It's stuffed with exhibits; some, are deliberately gory, like the dungeon and torture chamber. Others detail the various ghosts which have been reported over the centuries.

The Church of St Peter, Chillingham

“A moderate walk in a quiet hidden valley on the edge of the Cheviot Hills taking in grazed farmland, riverside woodland, and open meadows”

The small market town of Wooler in Glendale is a popular centre for exploring the Cheviot Hills. It lies by a stream called the Wooler Water part of which is also known, as 'Happy Valley'. This walk starts at the confluence of the Harthope and Carey Burns which rise in the Cheviots and join to create Wooler Water. The Harthope Valley was formed by a geological fault and the remote Harthope Linn waterfall can be found by continuing past the start of the walk and up this picturesque, tranquil valley.

Coldgate Water in the woods

walk
5

Happy Valley

Meadow beside Coldgate Water

Plan your walk

DISTANCE: 4 miles (6.5km)

TIME: 2 hours

START/END: NT976249 South of Wooler on the minor road to Langleeford, park in a grassy area to the right, just north of the Carey Burn

TERRAIN: Moderate; muddy sections

MAPS: OS Explorer OL 16; OS Landranger 75

Route instructions

A Walk on along the road, towards the bridge across the Carey Burn. Cross this and then turn hard left, beside a fence; then left again, through a gate; and then right, across a footbridge over the Harthope Burn. Climb the slope beyond and walk on, with an oak wood spreading down the valley slope to the right. Take care on this section as it can be quite muddy.

B When a fence comes in from the right, go round it and cut right, on a well-trodden path. Continue in this direction until a dyke and a line of hawthorns cross ahead. Continue straight on and keep right of a large pond heading for a stile up the slope. Then cross a small footbridge and over the protected barbed wire after which the path is indistinct so bear left across the slope aiming for the top edge of a wood. If you are lucky you may see a brown hare leaping through the bracken on this hillside.

C Head right, slightly uphill, and follow waymarkers onto a good track to reach North Middleton.

D Once the track reaches the road turn left, as far as the ford over the burn. To the left of the ford is a footbridge. Cross this and turn left, along a clear track through dense conifer and broad-leaved woodland by the burn side.

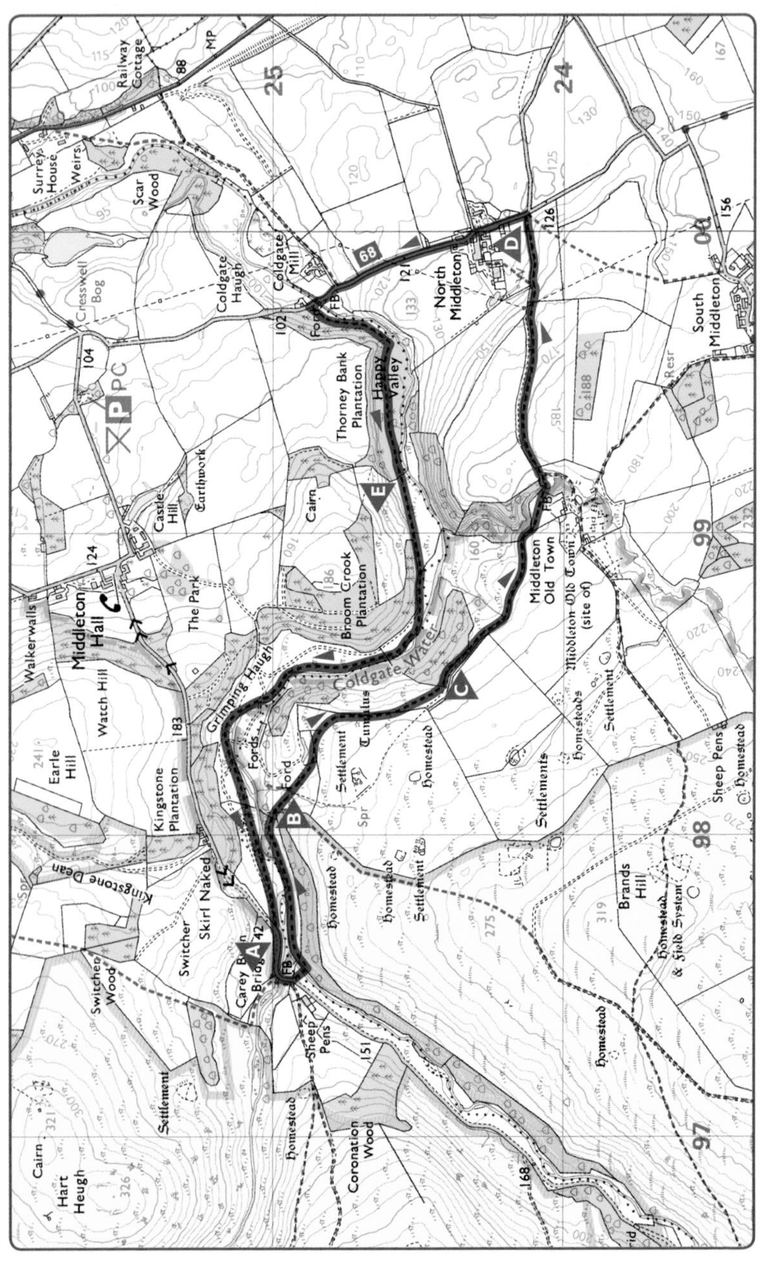

Surrey House
Weirs
Scar Wood
Railway Cottage
Cresswell Bog
Coldgate Haugh
Coldgate Mill
FB
Ford
68
North Middleton
South Middleton
Thorney Bank Plantation
Happy Valley
Castle Hill
Earthwork
PC
Middleton Hall
Walkerwalls
The Park
Watch Hill
Earle Hill
Cairn
Broom Crook Plantation
Grimping Haugh
Coldgate Water
Tumulus
Fords
Settlement
Homestead
Middleton Old Town
Middleton Old Town (site of)
Settlements
Homesteads
Sheep Pens
Kingstone Plantation
Kingstone Dean
Skirl Naked
Switcher
Switcher Wood
Carey Burn Bridge
Brands Hill
Homestead & Field System
Coronation Wood
Hart Heugh
Resr
Spr
A
B
C
D
E
25
24
99
98
97

Happy Valley

E When the woodland ends continue across the grazing land on the flood plain, back to the bridge. Some sections are well used by cattle and can be very muddy. At one point the burn swings to the north, and it is necessary to follow a path through the gorse scrub up to the right.

Footbridge over Coldgate Water

“Encompassing a pretty coastal village, a muddy estuary, riverside farmland and a fine sandy beach this a lovely varied walk”

Alnmouth is a fine sea-side village on a peninsula between the tidal mud of the Aln Estuary and the sands of Alnmouth Bay. In medieval times it was an important port, but now it is simply an unspoilt haven for small boats.

Alnmouth village at low tide

Alnmouth

Lesbury church

Plan your walk

DISTANCE: 4 miles (6.5km)

TIME: 2 hours

START/END: NU246103 Alnmouth

TERRAIN: Easy

MAPS:
OS Explorer 332;
OS Landranger 81

Route instructions

A Walk down to the southern end of the village and turn right along Riverside Road. Continue on this road until, just beyond a children's playground, a path (signed 'Lovers Walk') to the left of a gate, cuts towards the mud-flats.

B Continue beside the mudflats to the Duchess's Bridge, then climb up onto the bridge and turn left. Walk on the pavement and then a gravel path running beside the road for about ¼ mile (0.5km). Go through a car park to the playing field ahead.

C Follow the right hand edge of this playing field to the corner and then continue on a path parallel to a row of houses which starts to the left. At the end of the row there is a gate, after which the path cuts half left, leading across a field to another gate. This leads to a road, and then to a bridge over the Aln.

D Cross the bridge and bear right diagonally across the riverside grass to the fields. Alternatively, for a quick diversion into Lesbury village follow the track straight on from the bridge and turn right along the road. When the B1339 cuts left, turn right down a lane opposite running between the houses to the riverside grassy area where a left turn leads to the fields.

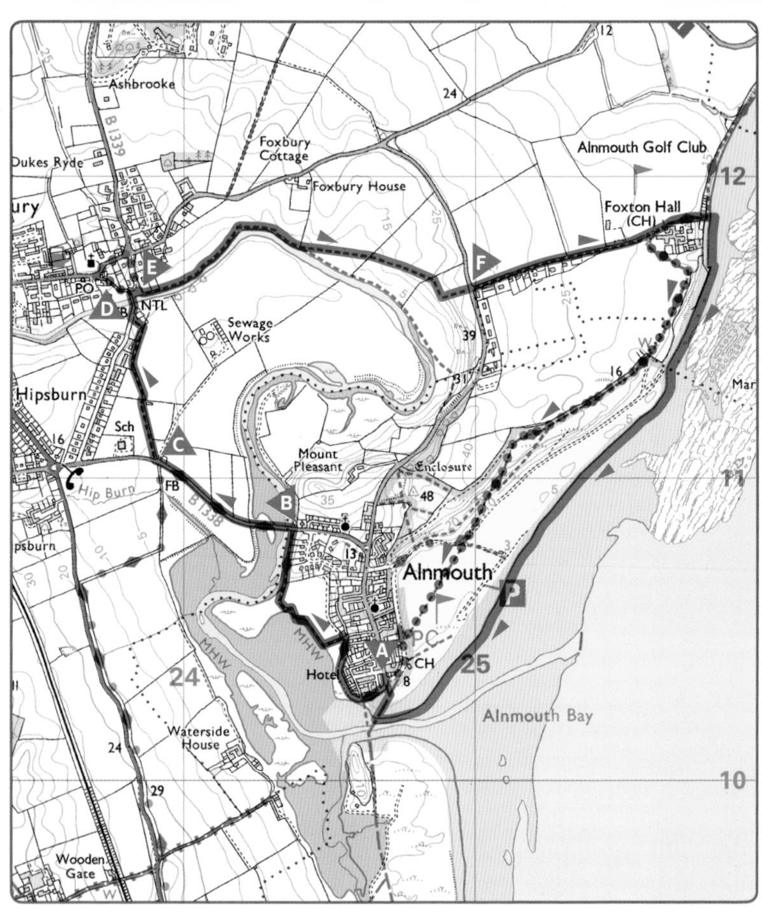

E Follow the path through three fields gradually veering away from the river before climbing the steep slope on the left to end up slightly to the right of a line of telegraph poles. Once at the top of the slope, cross a stile, and the road beyond, and walk down the driveway into Alnmouth Golf Club, directly opposite.

F Follow the drive down to the club house. When a wall starts on the left-hand side, walk down a path to the left of it, leading down to a fine sandy shore, and then turn right to return to Alnmouth. If the sea is rough use an alternative route by turning right immediately in front of the clubhouse and follow the cliff path back to Alnmouth passing between two golf greens on the way.

Alnmouth

Alnmouth Beach and mouth of the Aln Estuary

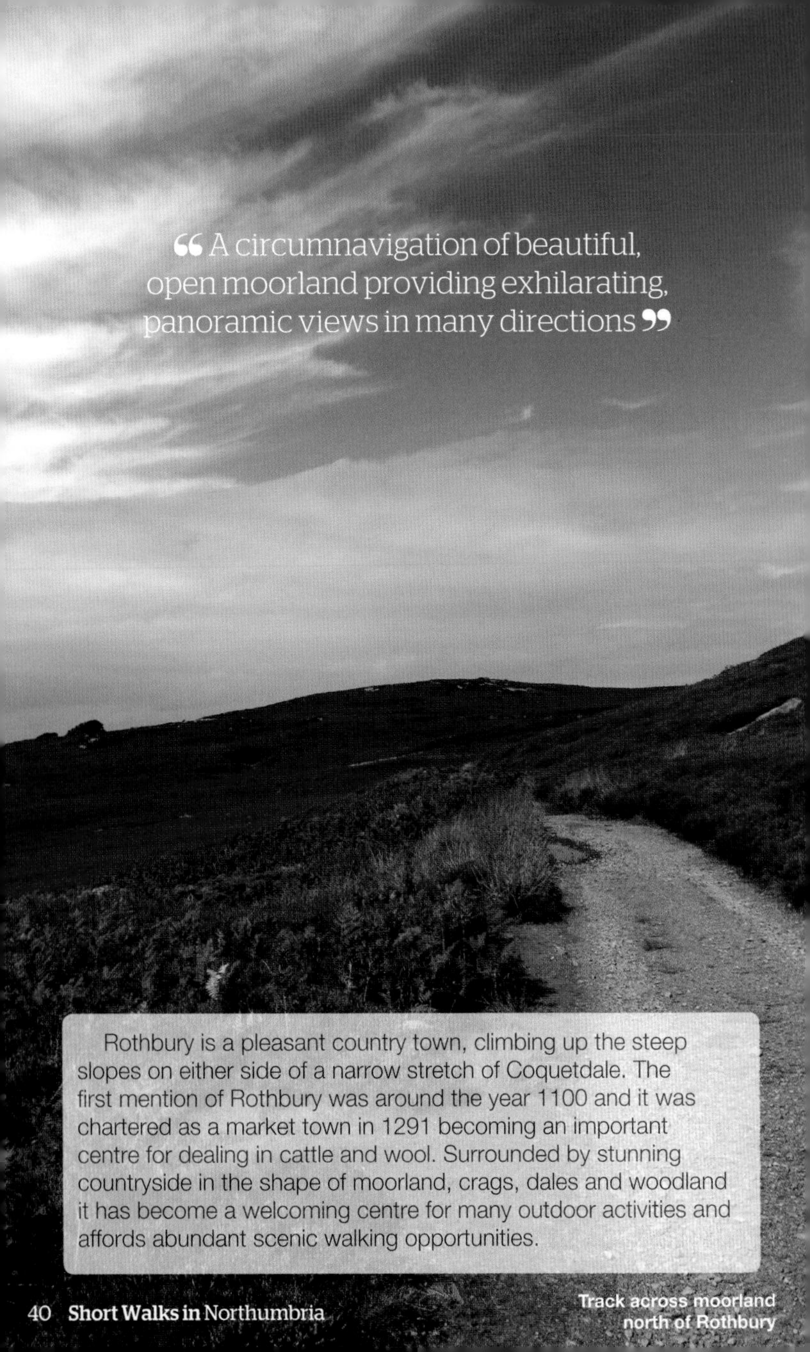

“A circumnavigation of beautiful, open moorland providing exhilarating, panoramic views in many directions”

Rothbury is a pleasant country town, climbing up the steep slopes on either side of a narrow stretch of Coquetdale. The first mention of Rothbury was around the year 1100 and it was chartered as a market town in 1291 becoming an important centre for dealing in cattle and wool. Surrounded by stunning countryside in the shape of moorland, crags, dales and woodland it has become a welcoming centre for many outdoor activities and affords abundant scenic walking opportunities.

Track across moorland north of Rothbury

Rothbury

Moorland cairn with views of Rothbury

Plan your walk

DISTANCE: 5 miles (6.5km)

TIME: 2½ hours

START/END: NU057017 Rothbury

TERRAIN: Moderate; one 500ft (150m) climb

MAPS: OS Explorer 332; OS Landranger 81

Route instructions

A Start from the centre of the town. Walk up the alley which runs from the High Street between the Co-Op and Millers of Stanley. When you reach a lane, turn left, then right after 55 yards (50m). Continue steeply upwards, along a path between hedges to join Hillside Road, on the northern edge of the town.

B On the far side of the road, a sign indicates a footpath to Cartington. Continue in the direction of this sign up Blaeberry Hill and as the road bends left continue straight ahead on a path between two fences. Then follow a rough path past the left hand edge of a wood and on to the moor.

C Cross a gravel track to join a track running across the moor towards a plantation.

D Cross a stile into this plantation and turn right along a grassy track. At a T-junction in the wood, turn right, down to Primrose Cottage on the edge of the trees.

E From the cottage, turn left on a clear track running along the edge of the plantation, signposted to 'Thropton and Rothbury'. Continue along this track. At one point it is crossed by another track: carry straight on through a gate and then through woodland.

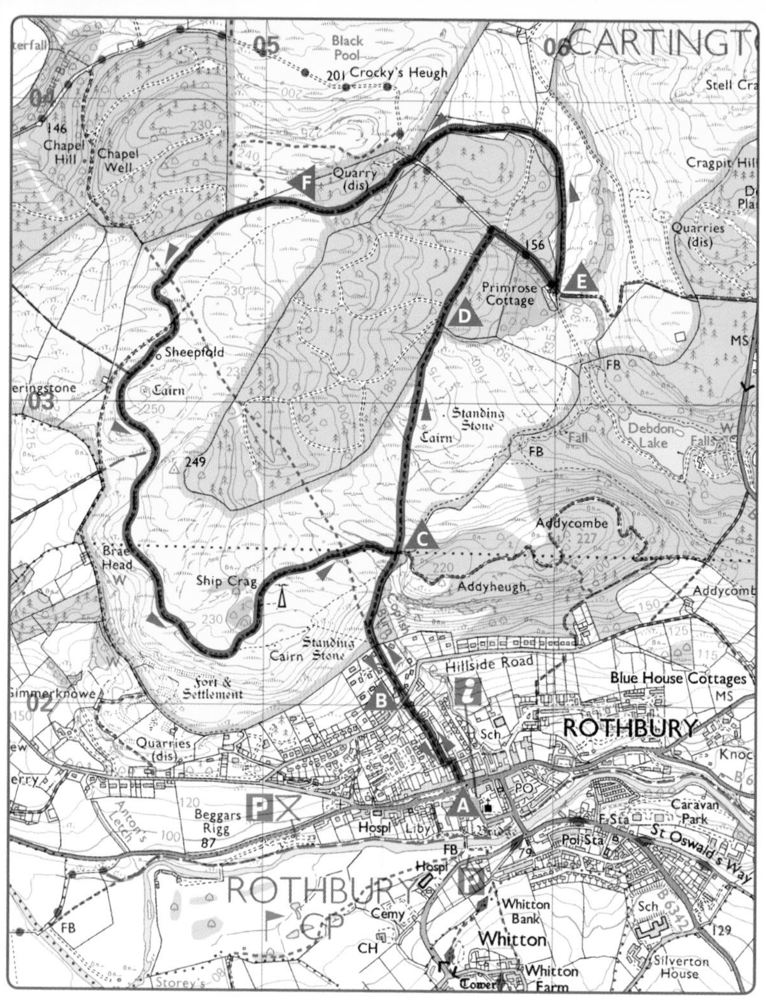

F At the far end of the wood the track emerges once more onto the moor. Initially it heads westwards, towards another plantation, but then it cuts to the south, winding across the moorland and providing fine views of Coquetdale and the Simonside Hills (see walk 8). Continue on this track until it rejoins the path from Rothbury, then turn right to return down to the town.

Rothbury

Rothbury village centre

“A choice of forest walks through conifer woodland emerging on a breathtaking ridge of open moorland with far-reaching views in all directions”

Rothbury is a fine old country town, in a narrow section of Coquetdale, pressed between a steep slope to the north (see walk 7) and the forestry covered slopes and ridges of the Simonside Hills to the south.

Path along Simonside Ridge

Simonside

Views of Rothbury from Simonside Ridge

Plan your walk

DISTANCE: Up to 4½ miles (7.25km)

TIME: 2½ hours

START/END: NZ037997 Simonside car park off the minor road south east of Great Tosson village

TERRAIN: Strenuous; one climb of 750ft (230m)

MAPS: OS Explorer OL 42; OS Landranger 81

Route instructions

1 There are two official signposted routes through the forest. One is a one-mile loop from the car park. The main route, waymarked in red, leads up to the pronounced rocky ridges which rise up above the forest to the south. These sandstone ridges are similar in composition and form to those in Thrunton Forest to the north.

A There is parking beside a display point with lots of information about local flora and fauna. Follow the red arrows westwards beyond a barrier. This track follows a winding route up through the conifers. It eventually meets the Simonside Ridge path, a sandstone slab path up and along a line of crags from which there are fine views of Rothbury and Thropton, and of the hills to the north of Coquetdale.

B There is one possible alteration to the path indicated. At Dove Crag, instead of following the forest walk back into the trees, continue along the ridge on the path to the Beacon Cairn. From there you can drop down to the car park marked on the map. The final descent is a brief section of St Oswald's Way, a 97-mile (156 km) walk between Holy Island and Hadrian's Wall.
Turn left along the road to return to the start of the walk.

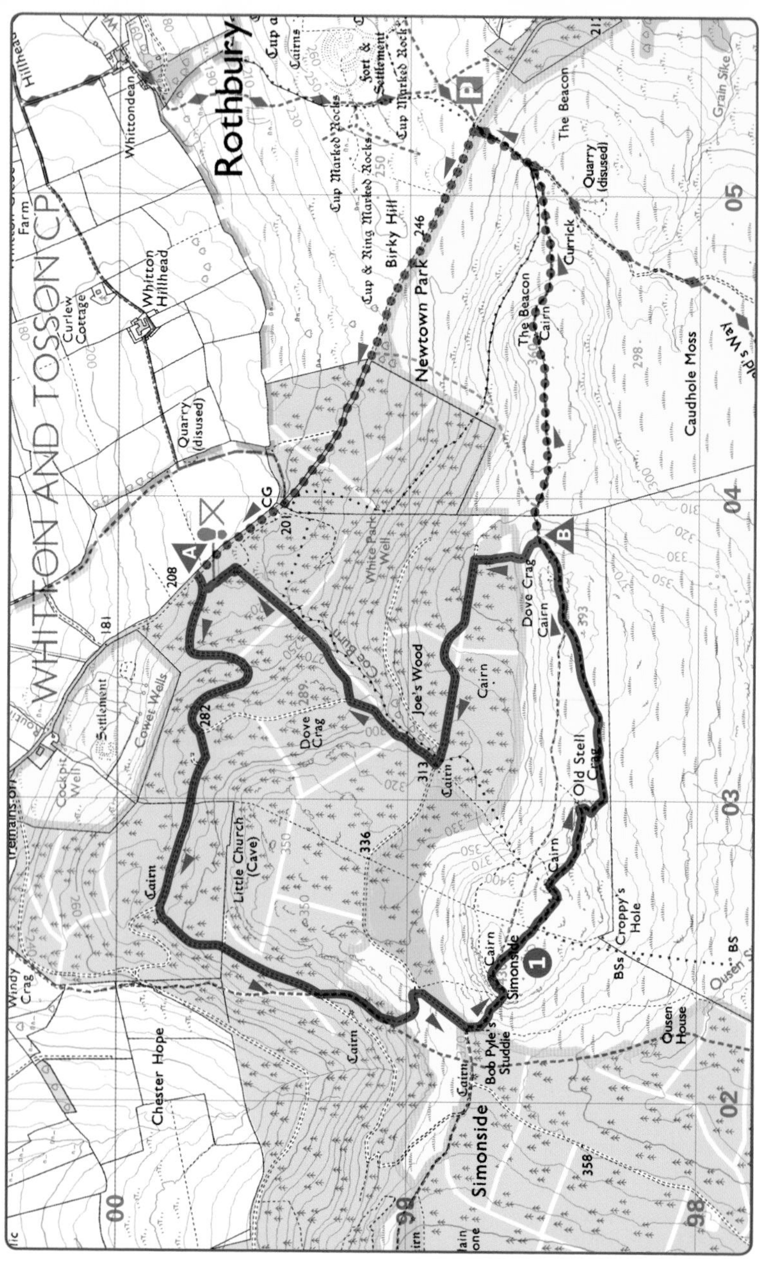
Rothbury
WHITTON AND TOSSON CP
Whittondean
Whitton Hillhead
Curlew Cottage
Quarry (disused)
Cup Marked Rocks
Cup & Ring Marked Rocks
Birky Hill
Newtown Park
The Beacon
Currick
Cairn
Caudhole Moss
Coe Burn
White Pack Well
Joe's Wood
Dove Crag
Settlement
Cowet Wells
Cockpit Well
Little Church (Cave)
Old Stell Crag
Croppy's Hole
Simonside
Bob Pyle's Studdie
Ousen House
Chester Hope
Windy Crag
CG
A
B
P
1

Simonside

Path along Simonside Ridge

“A linear path up a deep, wooded glen, crisscrossing a bubbling burn towards a dramatic waterfall”

The small town of Bellingham (pronounced 'Belling-jum') is the main centre for a large area around the valley of the River North Tyne (on which it sits), Redesdale and the massive Kielder Forest.

The Hareshaw Burn meets the River North Tyne in Bellingham and not far upstream is the delightful Hareshaw Linn waterfall. This Site of Special Scientific Interest is home to rare ferns and lichen as well as red squirrel, great spotted woodpecker and Daubenton's bat.

Woodland path approaching Hareshaw Linn

Hareshaw Linn

Footbridge over Hareshaw Burn

Plan your walk

DISTANCE: 3 miles (5km) there and back

TIME: 1½ hours

START/END: NY840834 Bellingham

TERRAIN: Easy

MAPS:
OS Explorer OL 42;
OS Landranger 80

Route instructions

A From the centre of the town, turn down the road signposted for 'Redesmouth'. The road crosses the Hareshaw Burn almost immediately. Cut left directly after the bridge on a road leading up to a car park on the edge of the town. From the car park, a signpost indicates the start of the footpath. The route is quite clear. It starts as a gravel track climbing through an area of open ground. Once past the ruins of the Hareshaw Ironworks you can choose the path beside the stream or the less muddy gravel track.

B Pass the picnic table area to enter the mixed woodland of the upper valley. In the woods the path alternates between running low down right beside the burn and higher sections giving views through the trees. After a while the path also winds back and forth across the burn on a sequence of footbridges before finally entering a rocky canyon at the head of the valley. The highlight of this glen is a fine waterfall called Hareshaw Linn of some 30ft (12m) dropping through the gap between two great blocks of stone. At the end of the path a small cave is cut into the rocky wall to the right, providing a dry viewing point of this dramatic scene.

C Return by the same route.

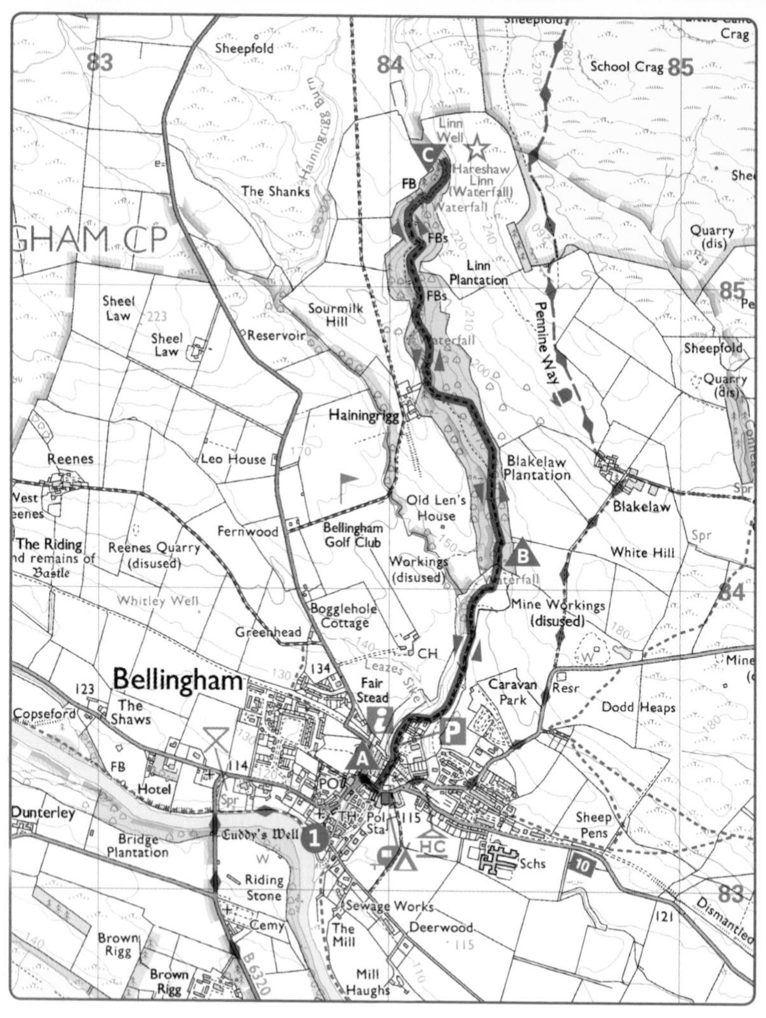

1 The most interesting building in the town is St Cuthbert's Church. The earliest sections date from the 13th century, but later additions were made in the early 17th and the 19th centuries. The place is very strongly built, with a heavy stone roof and slit windows. The cannon balls found in the roof during its reconstruction are evidence that, this close to the Border, a building had to be strong to survive.

Hareshaw Linn

Hareshaw Linn

“A steeply undulating path running beside sections of Hadrian's Wall with magnificent views either side of this historic ridge”

When Hadrian's Wall was completed, in AD163, it stretched 73 miles (117km), from the Solway Firth in the west to the Tyne estuary in the east. For most of the following two centuries, it was to be the northern boundary of the Roman Empire in Britain.

The builders' search for the most easily defended route for their wall led them across the bleak land to the north of the River South Tyne, where they were able to utilise the outcrops of the Whin Sill, a recurring geological feature in Northumbria which produces a series of steep crags. Thus, the wall is not only a relic of great archaeological interest, it is also scenically fascinating.

Hadrian's Wall

Hadrian's Wall from field near King's Wicket

Route instructions

A This route starts from the car park on the brow of the ridge at Steel Rigg just north of Once Brewed on the B6318. Walk east from the car park. Follow the path beside the wall along the crags of Steel Rigg and through the woods above Crag Lough.

B At the far end of the lough, the path crosses the track leading back to Hotbank Farm. At this point it is possible to double back to the car park, by turning right down the track for a short distance, and then right again at the sign for a footpath, along the Roman road. This makes a walk of around 3 miles (5km). Otherwise, continue (leaving Hotbank beyond a dyke to the left) along the wall for a further mile (1.6km) to the great ruined fort at Housesteads (fee on entry).

1 Housesteads is the most well known fort on Hadrian's Wall and known to the Romans as 'Vercovicium', 'the place of effective fighters'. Added to the wall around AD124 the site covers an area of about 5 acres (2ha) and it was garrisoned by approximately 1,000 infantry. The overall fort the layout changed very little during its 3 centuries of occupation but the internal buildings went through various stages of modification evident in the remains exposed today.

Plan your walk

DISTANCE: 3–7½ miles (5–12km)

TIME: Up to 4 hours

START/END: NY750676 Steel Rigg car park

TERRAIN: Moderate/ Strenuous; with steep undulations

MAPS:
OS Explorer OL 43;
OS Landranger 86

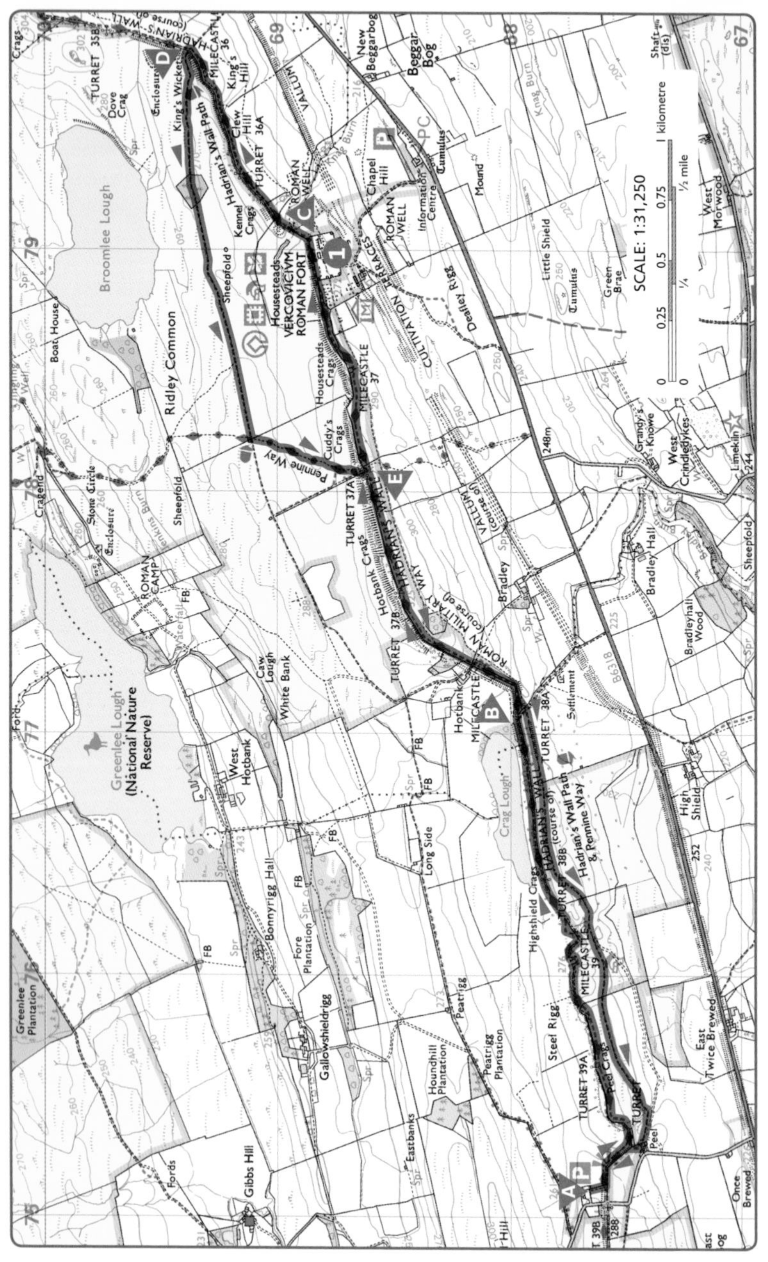

SCALE: 1:31,250
0 0.25 0.5 0.75 1 kilometre
0 ¼ ½ mile
Broomlee Lough
Greenlee Lough
(National Nature Reserve)
Ridley Common
HOUSESTEADS
VERCOVICIVM
ROMAN FORT
HADRIAN'S WALL
Hadrian's Wall Path
Pennine Way
Crag Lough
Highshield Crags
Hotbank Crags
Housesteads Crags
Cuddy's Crags
Kennel Crags
King's Wicket
King's Hill
Clew Hill
Sewingshields Crags
MILECASTLE 37
MILECASTLE 39
TURRET 37A
TURRET 37B
TURRET 38A
TURRET 38B
TURRET 39A
TURRET 36A
TURRET 35B
VALLUM
ROMAN MILITARY WAY (course of)
CULTIVATION TERRACES
ROMAN WELL
ROMAN CAMP
Information Centre
Chapel Hill
Beggar Bog
New Beggarbog
Deafley Rigg
Little Shield
Green Brae
West Morwood
Grandy's Knowe
West Crindledykes
Limekiln
Bradley
Bradley Hall
Bradleyhall Wood
High Shield
East Twice Brewed
Once Brewed
Peel
Peel Crags
Steel Rigg
Peatrigg
Peatrigg Plantation
Houndhill Plantation
Eastbanks
Gallowshieldrigg
Fore Plantation
Bonnyrigg Hall
Long Side
West Hotbank
Hotbank
Caw Lough
White Bank
Greenlee Plantation
Gibbs Hill
Fords
Boat House
Sheepfold
Stone Circle
Cragend
Dove Crag
Mound
Settlement
Tumulus
B6318
A
B
C
D
E
1

Hadrian's Wall

C▶ Continue along the right-hand side of the wall for a further ½ mile (1km) beyond Housesteads, dropping down from the steep summit of King's Hill until a stile appears to the left beside a gate named 'King's Wicket'. Looking westwards from the stile, the wall runs along a series of crags to the left, there is a marshy hollow beneath the crags, and, to the right, a ridge runs parallel to the wall.

D▶ Turn left over the stile and follow the indistinct route over the marshy ground towards a small copse. Continue through the trees where the path can be muddy and head towards the Pennine Way enjoying fine views of the parallel ridge of crags to the left. At the intersection with the Pennine Way, turn left and climb uphill to return to the wall.

E▶ Return to Steel Rigg along the original route to the right. When approaching Crag Lough there is the option to return by an alternative route as described in B▶.

Hadrian's Wall looking east to Crag Lough

“A circuit through exhilarating moorland and hill-farmland around an old lead-mining settlement”

Allenheads sits at the very head of beautiful East Allen Dale; 1300ft (400m) above sea level. It is a tiny village, originally built to house people working in the lead mines of the area. There is a Heritage Centre in the village explaining its history, while the surrounding moorland is littered with the surviving traces of the industry.

Ruin on hillside above East Allen Dale

Allenheads

Currick on moor above Allenheads

Plan your walk

DISTANCE: 5 miles (8km)

TIME: 2½ hours

START/END: NY859453 Allenheads

TERRAIN: Moderate; one climb of 600ft (180m)

MAPS: OS Explorer OL 31; OS Landranger 87

Route instructions

A Start from the centre of the village and head off up Rookhope Road. Follow this road as it climbs steeply for about ¾ mile (1.2km). A short distance after a cattle grid a clear track cuts off the road to the left. This leads past a quarry which once provided stone roof slates (an attractive feature of many of the buildings along this walk) up to the stone curricks on Dodd End.

B Follow the track right from the curricks (remains of stone sheep enclosures), and continue with a dyke to the left. The track traverses the side of the hill behind a string of fine ruins. There are views to the old mine workings across the dale.

C Pass behind Byerhope Farm then continue in the same direction until another track appears ahead. Turn right at this junction marked by a cairn and follow this track for a short distance up onto a ridge.

D Look out for a post with arrows marking the start of the bridleway on the left, back down to the road. Follow these posts which mark the descent towards a row of cottages. Cross the road at the bottom and walk down the minor road opposite as it zigzags down to the river.

E Cross the bridge to the right of the ford and follow the road to the left. When it breaks to the right, continue

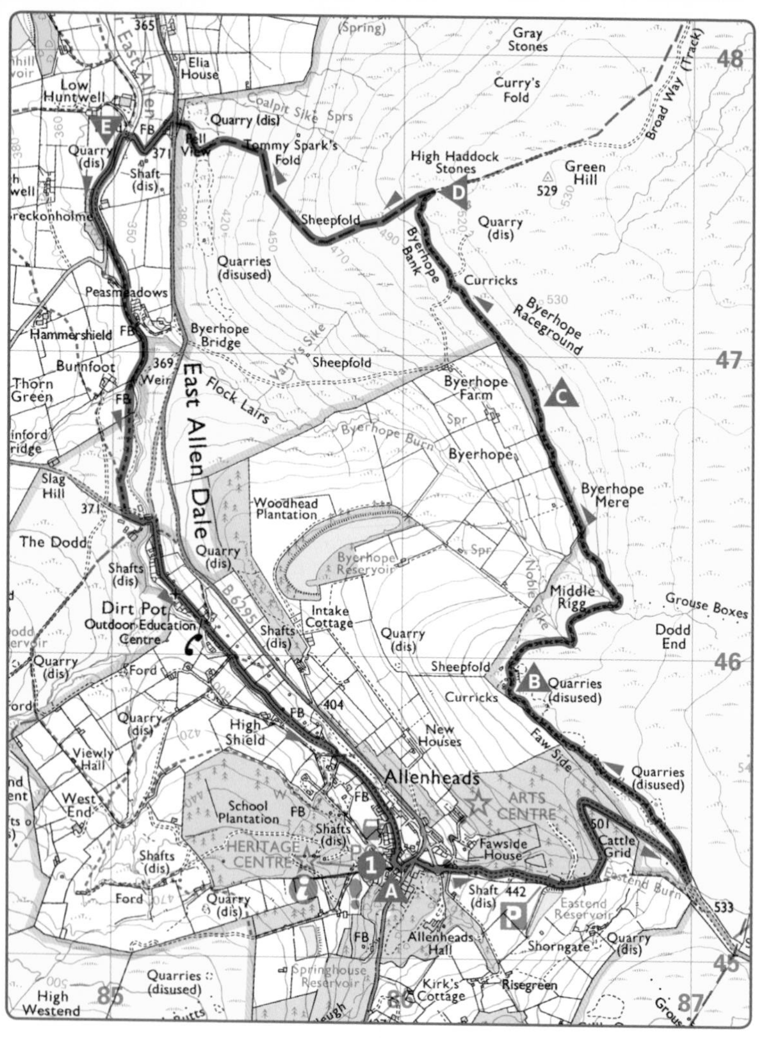

along the riverside footpath. This eventually joins the road once again. Cross the river and turn right to return to Allenheads.

1 In the village centre is a Heritage Centre depicting the lead-mining past of the village. This houses the important Armstrong water engine and a restored blacksmith's shop as well as a welcome café.

Allenheads

Path beside River East Allen

“This loop has a wonderful mixture of scenery from an enchanting village, to a peaceful valley, sweeping moorland and a delightful leafy riverside”

The village of Blanchland, though only small, is one of the finest in Northumbria, and its pastoral elegance comes as something of a surprise amidst the bleak moors and hills of the area. The greater part of the settlement was built in the 18th century, on the site of a 12th century abbey; but the great gate-house on one side of the square is older: it dates from the 15th century.

Ruin of an old lead mine in Shildon

Blanchland

Blanchland gate-house and post office

Plan your walk

DISTANCE: 3½ miles (5.5km)

TIME: 1¾ hours

START/END: NY964504 Blanchland

TERRAIN: Moderate; gradual climb of 350ft (110m)

MAPS:
OS Explorer 307;
OS Landranger 87

Route instructions

A Park in the car park on the northern edge of the village and start walking up the metalled road beside the Shildon Burn; through woodland at first, but later through open farmland. As the farmland turns to moorland, the views across the Derwent Vale become more spectacular.

1 At one point, opposite Shildon, there is the ruin of an old lead mine on private land on the left-hand side of the road. The village of Blanchland was originally built to house lead miners.

B Follow the road up to Pennypie. When a track cuts right, up to the house, carry straight on through a gate in the wall. Then turn left at a path signed 'Baybridge', across a footbridge over the burn and on along a clear track through heather moorland. Watch for red grouse and curlew along this stretch.

C Follow the track until it joins a metalled road, then cut left down to the road. Looking across the valley, it is possible to see the chimneys of the old lead mines on the moors over towards Weardale.

D Turn right along the road until, just before it crosses the River Derwent, a footpath cuts off to the left, signposted for 'Blanchland'. Follow the uneven path along the riverside, through a narrow

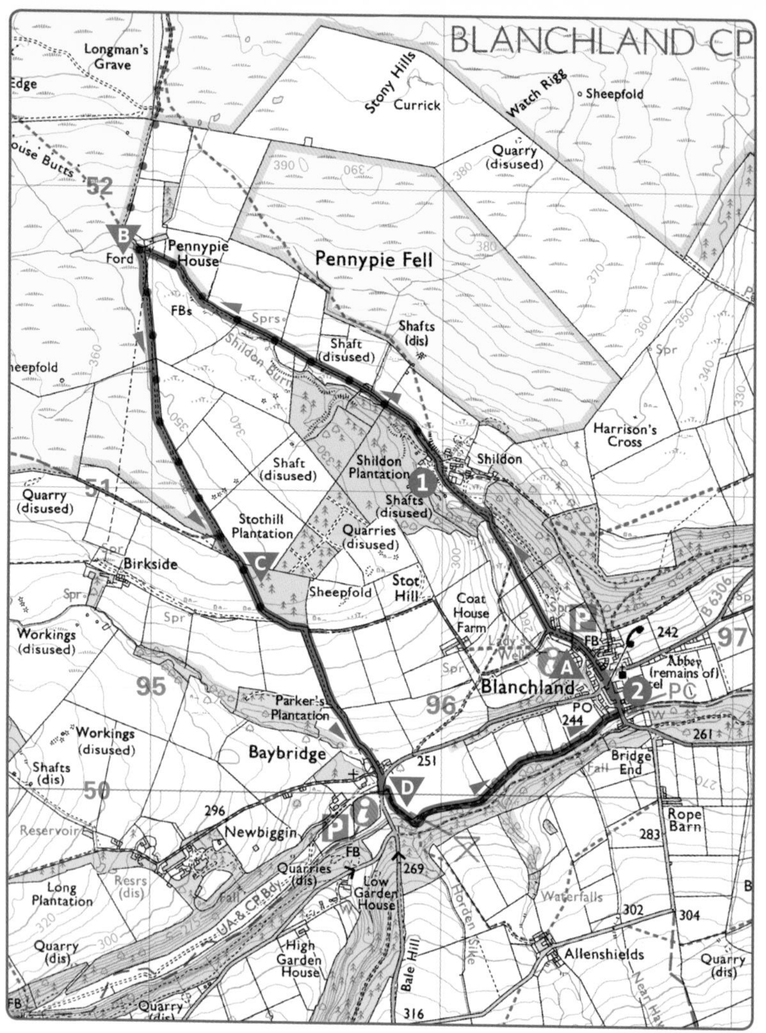

band of mixed woodland, back to the village.

2 Blanchland lies in the Upper Derwent Valley in the North Pennines Area of Outstanding Natural Beauty. This historic collection of buildings form the centrepiece of an estate owned by a charitable trust. The unspoilt qualities of this conservation village make it a frequent setting for 18th-century period films.

Blanchland

Signpost on Birkside Fell

“Rough paths and clear tracks leading through fine mixed woodland”

A historic market town on the banks of the River Tyne, Hexham has many sites of interest. Its railway station is one of the oldest in the world, operational since 1835 and the oldest 'Gaol' in the country now tells the story of Hexham's past. The dominating building, however, is the 13th century Hexham Abbey built on the site of an earlier church and monastery dating back to AD 674. The Battle of Hexham in 1464 was regarded to be one of the decisive events in the War of the Roses but the exact location of this skirmish is in question. The popular view is that it took place on the Hexham Levels but an alternative suggestion is that Swallowship Wood was the more likely site being strategically placed on the crest of Swallowship Hill along the southern edge of this walk.

View looking north from path to Hexham

Hexham

Park Wood

Plan your walk

DISTANCE: 3½ miles (5.5km)

TIME: 1¾ hours

START/END: NY944630 B6306 on the southeast edge of Hexham

TERRAIN: Easy; 250ft (80m) undulating

MAPS: OS Explorer OL 43; OS Landranger 87

Route instructions

A Park to the west of the road, near the entrance to Dukeshouse Wood Outdoor Centre. Walk back down the road for about 400yds (0.3km). Turn right down the road signposted for Fellside.

B After a row of cottages on the left, bear right off the road at the signpost for the footpath to Duke's House, into an area of mixed woodland. There are a number of paths through the wood, and it is important to stick to the main one. This leads up a slope, bearing left along a felled, flatter section, then cutting hard right and running straight up (with a field to the left) to a junction with another track.

C Walk straight across the track and through a gap in the fence opposite, then bear slightly left along a well-trodden path. After a short distance, another track cuts across ahead; walk straight across this and continue beyond. At a split, follow the path sign left. The path splits again when it reaches a fence – walk left, along the line of the fence, and follow it down to the corner of a field; then cut left within wood, over a stream, then bear right, into a wood of pine trees.

D Take the right-hand path through the wood and when a gully appears ahead, keep above and to the left of it, on a path which leads

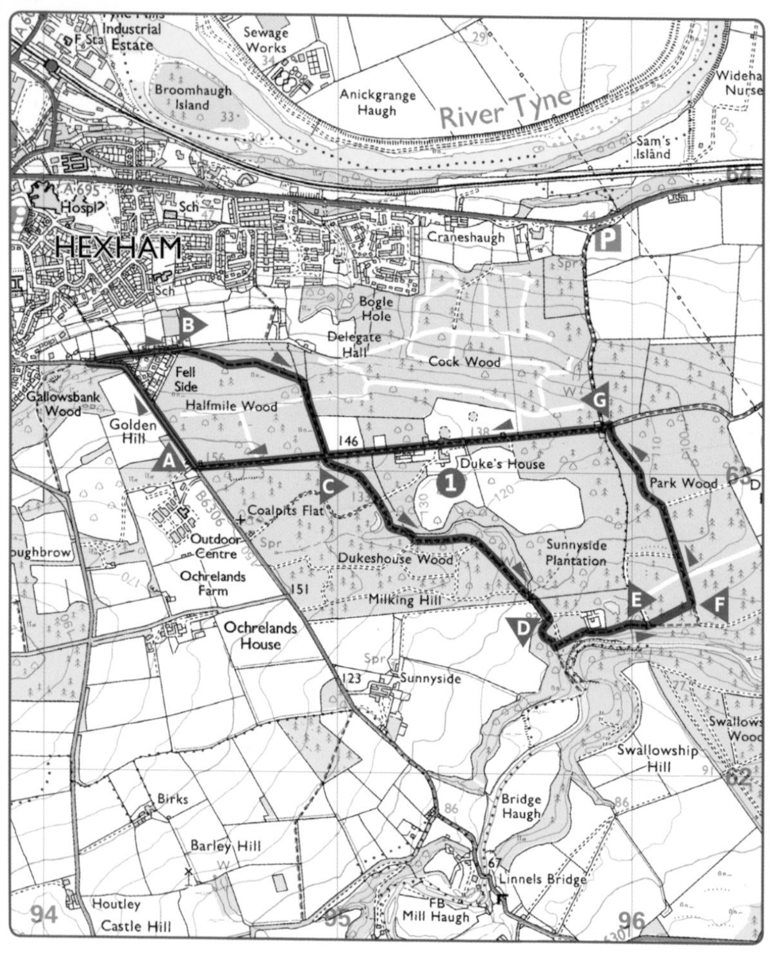

through an oak wood above the river.

E This path shortly crosses another, smaller gully. Bear slightly to the left across this, up a slope and through a gap in a crumbling wall, and continue on the track beyond. A track soon cuts off to the left. Ignore this and carry straight on.

F Continue until a T-junction is reached, then cut left and follow a clear track up hill to a further junction.

G Turn left and follow a clear path which then becomes a track past the Duke's House and back to the B6306.

Hexham

1 Dukes House or 'the house of a thousand chimneys' is one of the largest neo-gothic country homes in Hexham. It's surrounded by a huge garden in the midst of extensive woodland and it was allegedly built on the site of a cottage where Henry Beaufort, 3rd Duke of Somerset, was captured in 1464 before being taken to Hexham and executed.

Rooftop of Duke's House

The little town of Wylam holds an unrivalled position in the history of the railways. The line between Wylam Colliery and the port of Lemington – 5 miles (8km) down the Tyne carried the early steam locomotive Puffing Billy, built in 1813 by the pioneer William Hedley; while, by coincidence, the greatest name in the early history of rail, George Stephenson – the designer of The Rocket – was born in a little cottage by the side of the line. This path follows the route of the old line, and passes Stephenson's birthplace.

Wylam

Information board about the Wylam Waggonway

Plan your walk

DISTANCE: 4½ miles (7km)

TIME: 2¼ hours

START/END: NZ118646 Wylam

TERRAIN: Easy

MAPS: OS Explorer 316; OS Landranger 88

Route instructions

A Park in the car park (once Wylam Station) close to the river. The path used for this route is part of a longer walkway, running from Newburn – 3 miles (5km) to the east – to Ovingham – 3 miles (5km) up river to the west.

For this walk, set off along the track signposted 'Stephenson's Cottage'and 'Newburn'.

B After ½ mile (1km), look out for an information board on the left detailing the history of the Wyalm Waggonway. After this the track passes Stephenson's Cottage, which is now owned by the National Trust and is open to the public for restricted periods (check with tourist offices for details). The track then continues between a golf course to the left and the tree-lined river to the right. Gradually, the track pulls away from the riverside, and, after a mile (1.6km), reaches a row of cottages.

1 Stephenson's Cottage was built around 1760 to accommodate mining families. George Stephenson was born here in 1781, where his whole family lived in the one room. After making his name at nearby Wylam colliery he went on to become an engineer and inventor who built the first public railway in the world to use steam locomotives. The cottage furnishings reflect the period of this

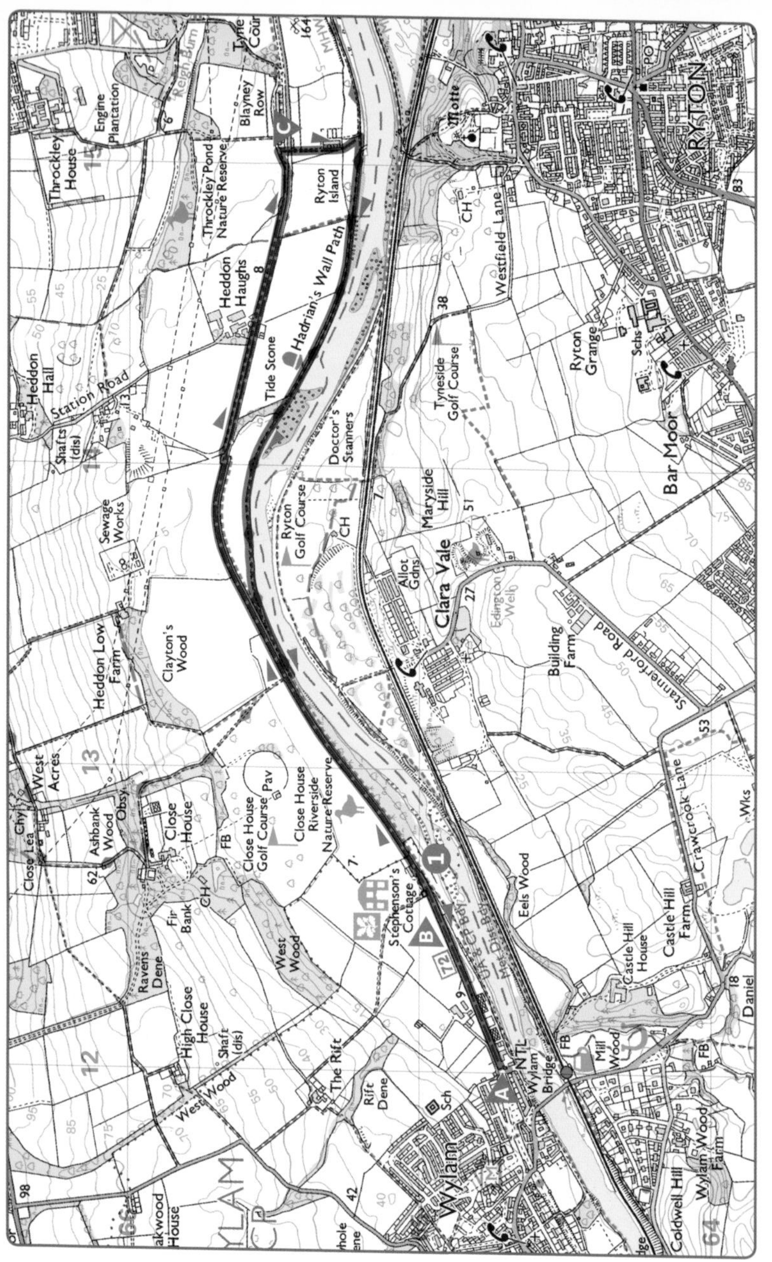

Throckley House
Engine Plantation
Reigh Burn
Tyne Court
Blayney Row
Throckley Pond Nature Reserve
Ryton Island
Heddon Haughs
Hadrian's Wall Path
Tide Stone
Heddon Hall
Station Road
Shafts (dis)
Sewage Works
Doctor's Stanners
Ryton Golf Course
CH
Motte
RYTON
PO
Westfield Lane
Tyneside Golf Course
Ryton Grange
Schs
Bar Moor
Maryside Hill
Clara Vale
Allot Gdns
Edington Well
Building Farm
Stannerford Road
Heddon Low Farm
Clayton's Wood
West Acres
Close Lea
Chy
Ashbank Wood
Obsy
Close House
Close House Golf Course
Pav
Close House Riverside Nature Reserve
FB
Fir Bank
Ravens Dene
High Close House
Shaft (dis)
West Wood
Stephenson's Cottage
UA & CP Bdy
Met Dist Bdy
Eels Wood
Castle Hill House
Castle Hill Farm
Crawcrook Lane
Wks
Daniel
The Rift
Rift Dene
Sch
Wylam
NTL
Wylam Bridge
Mill Wood
Coldwell Hill
Wylam Wood Farm
WYLAM

great rail pioneer, often referred to as the 'Father of Railways'.

C A mile (1.6km) further on down the track is the town of Newburn but, for this route, turn right at the cottages. This track leads in front of another terrace down to the river. Turn right along a paved path which soon becomes rough following the side of the Tyne – tidal as far up river as Wylam – to rejoin the original track.

Stephenson's Cottage

“Three signposted forest walks on good tracks through beautiful mixed woodland within which are a variety of natural and industrial heritage sites”

Chopwell Wood is a fine, mixed forestry wood on the northern slopes above the River Derwent. The existence of the wood is recorded as early as the 12th century, when it was a part of the estates belonging to the Bishops of Durham. It is now in the ownership of the Forestry Commission but is a somewhat more interesting place than many other commercial woods, having a large number of broad-leaved trees interspersed amongst the conifers. This allows more air and light into the forest and encourages the undergrowth.

walk 15

Chopwell Wood

Plan your walk

DISTANCE: 1½ – 4½ miles (1–5km)

TIME: ¾ – 2¼ hours

START/END: NZ137584 Chopwell Wood car park off the B6315 at Hooker Gate

TERRAIN: Easy / Moderate; undulating

MAPS: OS Explorer 307; OS Landranger 88

Route instructions

A On the B6315 at Hooker Gate, turn down a minor road leading to a car park in the forest from which there are three differently coloured, signposted walks. The two longer routes lead to a point giving views of the River Derwent through the trees and the River Walk continues along the top of the valley for a while, passing above a fine oak wood covering the slope down to the river. The trees in this part of the wood were planted after the Napoleonic Wars of the early 19th century, to replace those which had been taken to build ships for the English fleet.

1 For the Old Railway Footpath (1½ miles (2.4km)) follow the signposted blue route along which can be found two restored coal wagons which once ran along the Chopwell & Garesfield Railway between 1896 and 1961 connecting the Chopwell Colliery to High Spen and from there on to the River Tyne.

2 For the River Walk (3½ miles (5.6km)) follow the red route along which is a sculpted bench commemorating the mining industry. Further along the path there are some 200 year old settling tanks that provided clean water for the Lintzford Paper Mill between 1785 and 1923. This was just one of several paper mills in the Derwent Valley operational during the 17th and 18th centuries.

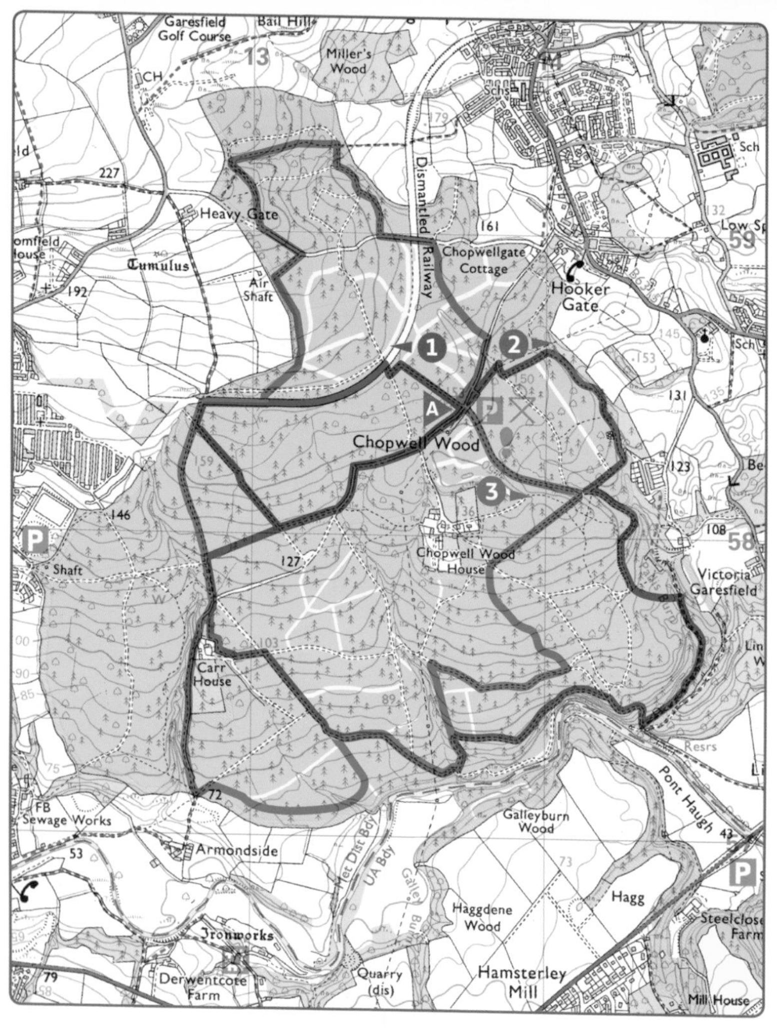

3 For the Boundary Walk (4½ miles (7.25km)) follow the signposted green route which has various points of interest including the site of the Chopwell Colliery fan which was used to exchange bad air for good air in the mine. The path also passes 'The Bomb Ponds' which were created in World War II but are now a conservation site. The other pond passed near the golf course was created in the early 20th century as a source of water for fighting forest fires.

Chopwell Wood

River Derwent through the trees in Chopwell Wood

“Good pathways through a mixed farming and industrial landscape with a section on the Lanchester Valley Way”

On the western outskirts of the cathedral city of Durham is Neville's Cross; the site of a battle in 1346 between David II of Scotland and an army of northern English lords. The English were victorious, and the Scottish king was imprisoned in London for 11 years.

Bearpark

Route instructions

A Park in Neville's Cross in a residential road off the busy A167 and start walking down Quarry House Lane – just to the north of the railway line. Follow this road until the gate; then cut left down a footpath along a wooded slope.

B After a short distance, there is a stile beside a gate leading into a field. Go over this and walk along a path to the right of the field. When the field ends continue along the path beside the River Browney. When a bridge over the river is reached, turn left across it and follow the road beyond up to a farm.

C A short distance after the farm, the track is crossed by a disused railway line. Turn right along this former section of line (between Durham and Lanchester) now designated the 'Lanchester Valley Way'.

D After ¾ mile (1.2km) proceed across a farm track and then over a minor road beyond it. Continue along the track, under the shadow of a hill on which are perched the terraces of the mining village of Bearpark. (Visible later on, from across the river).

E After a further ¾ mile (1.2km), the track is crossed by another track. The Lanchester Valley path continues straight ahead, but for this route, cut right; down across the River

Plan your walk

DISTANCE: 4½ miles (7.25km)

TIME: 2¼ hours

START/END: NZ260422 Neville's Cross

TERRAIN: Moderate

MAPS: OS Explorer 308; OS Landranger 88

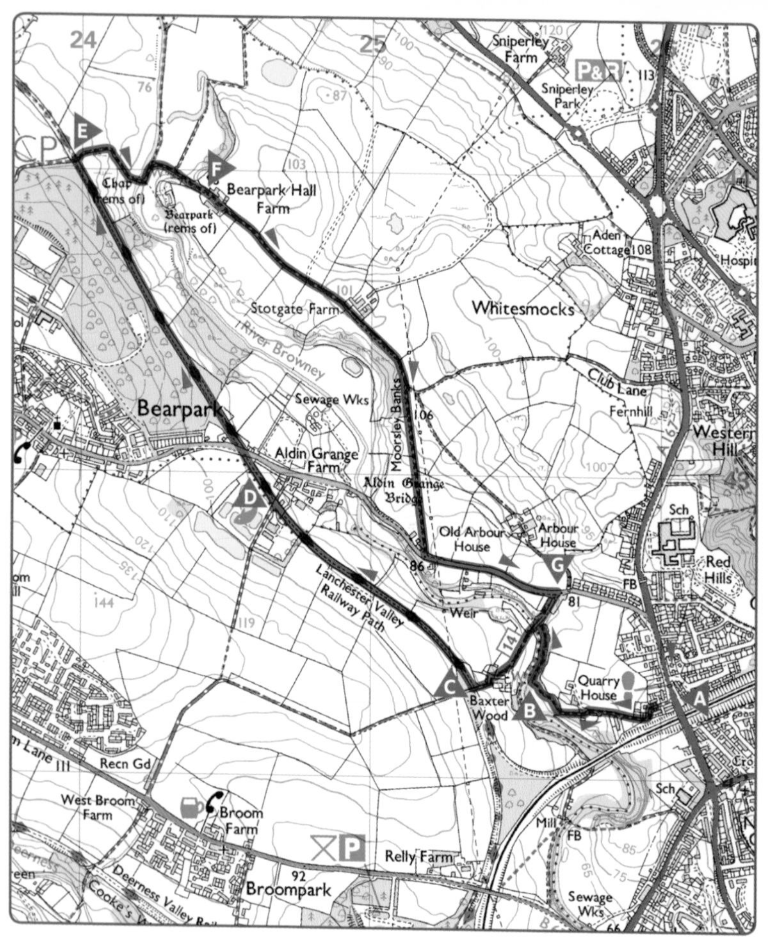

Browney, past the slight ruins of the old Bishops' residence of Beau Repaire on a mound by the river, and up the short slope.

F A good track leads past two farms with great views across the River Browney Valley to Bearpark (a corruption of 'Beau Repaire') before gradually dropping down to the road.

Turn left along the road (Tollhouse Road).

G Before you reach housing on your left, follow a cycleway sign right towards Lanchester and Consett. This takes you down to a bridge. Turn left onto the path before the bridge and retrace your route to Neville's Cross.

Bearpark

View northeast from
Bearpark Hall Farm track

“A riversde path through attractive riverside woodland returning on a higher ridge beside pleasant open farmland”

This route enjoys a small section of the Teesdale Way which is a long distance path (100 miles (160km)) running between the North Sea and the Pennines. The town of Barnard Castle is the attractive, historic ‘capital’ of Teesdale and draws many visitors but only a few minutes walking leads to a tranquil path beside the River Tees.

River Tees from a footbridge

Barnard Castle

Ruins of Barnard Castle

Plan your walk

DISTANCE: 4 miles (6.5km)

TIME: 2 hours

START/END: NZ049166 Barnard Castle

TERRAIN: Moderate; river path section can be difficult during or after high rainfall

MAPS:
OS Explorer OL 31;
OS Landranger 92

Route instructions

A Walk down the right-hand side of the church in the centre of town. Behind this building there is a grassy space, on the far side of which are the ruins of 12th century Barnard Castle (fee on entry). Bear right along a tarmac road which gradually drops down to the bank of the River Tees.

B After a short distance a bridge cuts left, across the river. Ignore this and take the path which crosses the footbridge over the little Percy Beck and then continues by the riverside.

C Follow this path through mixed woodland, past the twin supports of a dismantled rail bridge, and then on, for a further mile (1.6km) or so, through a pleasant rocky gorge to a small meadow by the riverside. Care should be taken on the riverside section during or after wet weather when the path may be difficult and exposed.

D Go through a gate into this meadow and follow the wall to the right for about 100yds (90m). When a gate appears to the right, go through it, then climb the wooded slope beyond to a fence by a field.

E Cross the fence and turn right. Continue through a succession of fields, keeping the woodland across the fence to the right until the circular walk yellow arrows

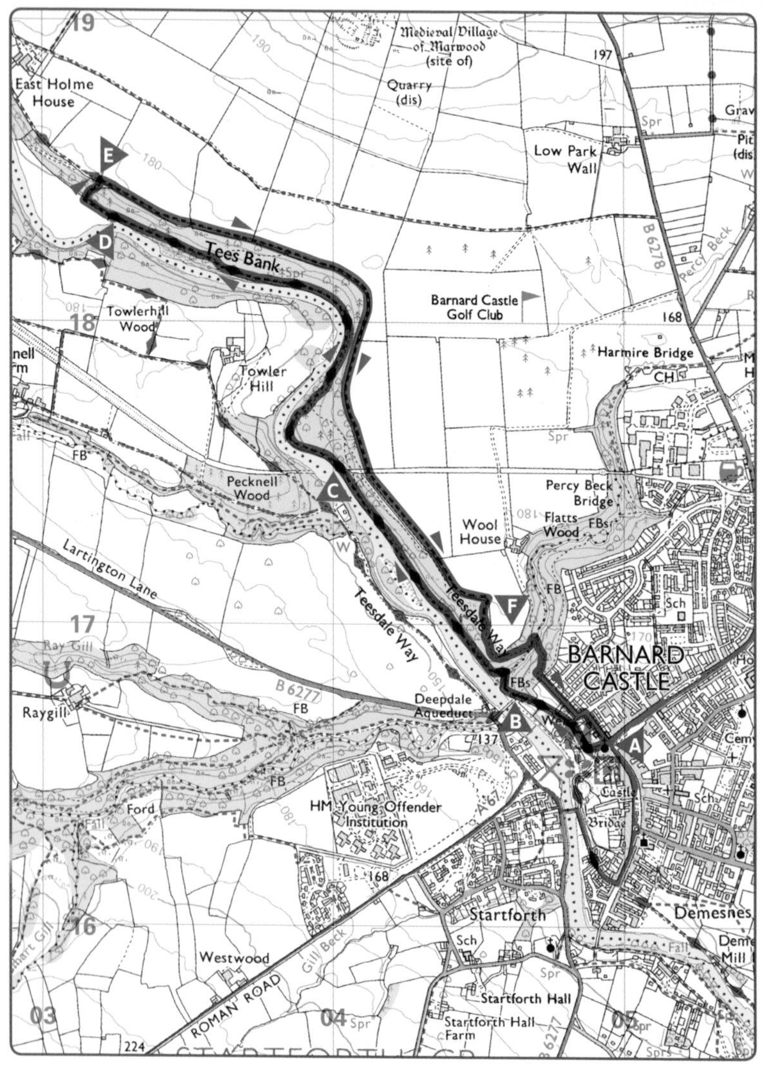

indicate to follow the path through a gate so a wall is now on the left. The route crosses the old railway line and then continues, providing lovely views of Barnard Castle (if foliage allows) and the surrounding farmland.

F Enter the woods and stay on the main path as it cuts through the trees, turning to the left and dropping to join a track adjacent to Percy Beck. On reaching the beck, cut left along a track and then right over the bridge signed 'Town Centre' and climb the steps beyond to reach Raby Avenue, leading down to the town centre.

View to the meadow by River Tees

“A gentle, low-level walk with idyllic river scenery and a striking ruined abbey”

Barnard Castle is a fine old market town situated at the eastern end of Teesdale. Its main features are the splendid Bowes Museum and Art Gallery, the ruin of its 12th century castle at the western end of the town (see walk 17), and the ruined Egglestone Abbey to the east.

Ruins of Egglestone Abbey

Egglestone Abbey

walk 18

River Tees at Barnard Castle

Plan your walk

DISTANCE: 3 miles (5km)

TIME: 1½ hours

START/END: NZ049166 Barnard Castle

TERRAIN: Easy

MAPS: OS Explorer OL 31; OS Landranger 92

Route instructions

A Start this walk from the Galgate – the broad street in the centre of Barnard Castle. Walk down to the end of the street nearest the castle and then turn left, down the Horsemarket. Carry straight on beyond the Market Cross (which acts as a roundabout), down The Back, then Thorngate and across the footbridge beyond.

B Climb the slope on the far side of the river upwards, and leftwards, then turn left along a road. When the road ends, go through a small gate to enter a caravan park. Turn right, and then go straight on. Keeping the outer row of caravans on your right, follow the park road as it bends left, then near right to leave the park. 220 yards (200m) before reaching the road, cut left across a stile into a field. Follow the left-hand edge of this field, and then continue across the left-hand side of three fields beyond to reach a tarmac road through a narrow stone opening.

C Cut left along the road, passing the picturesque ruins of the 12th century Egglestone Abbey which are well worth a visit. Continue along the road for ¼ mile (0.4km) and then cut left, across the small road bridge over the river.

1 Egglestone Abbey ruins give a good impression of the abandoned

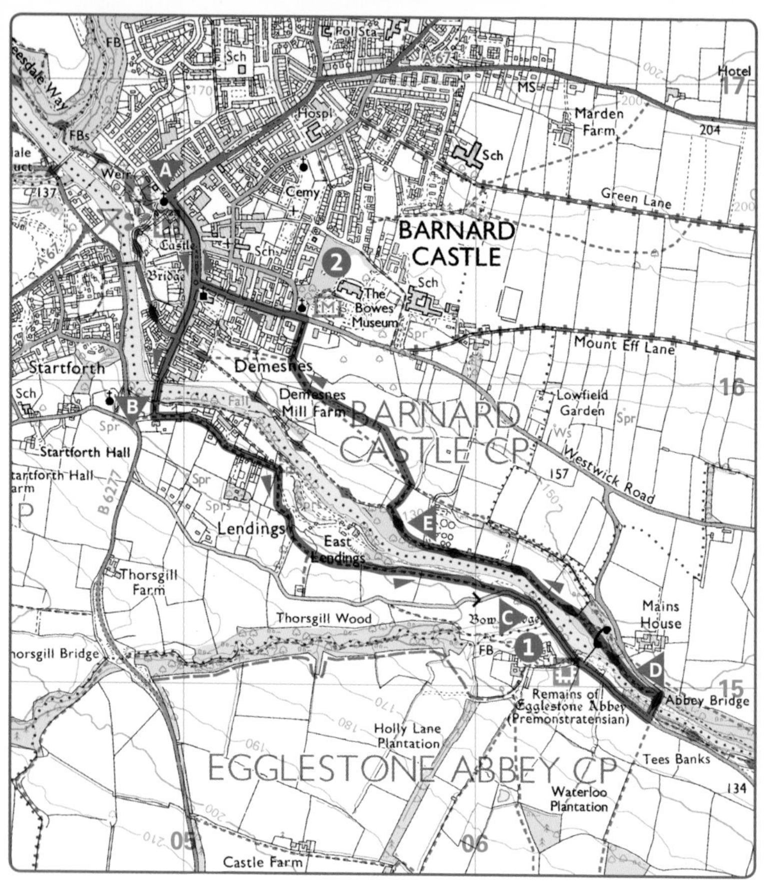

Premonstratensian monastery founded in the late 12th century. The founders undertook preaching and pastoral work in the region and wore a white habit thus becoming known as the 'White Canons'.

D Just over the bridge cut left, off the road, through a wall, onto a rough path which leads through dense woodland down to the riverside, where the trees give way on the right to open grazing land.

E Once the riverside path has passed the high fencing around the sewage works, gradually curve right across a field towards a small stone ruin. On reaching this building cut right, up the hill towards a stile. Cross the stile and bear left to follow the path around a sports pitch with views of the grand Bowes Museum

Egglestone Abbey

building to the right. Go through the gate in the far corner of the field, turn right up a walled lane and then left at the road to return to the town centre or right to visit the Bowes Museum.

2 The grand building of the Bowes Museum houses internationally significant collections of art. The structure was built in the 19th century by John and Joséphine Bowes who's passion for a wide range of arts led them to collect 15,000 objects from all over Europe between 1862 and 1874. Items varied from paintings and ceramics to textiles and furniture but sadly neither John or Joséphine lived to see the museum open in 1892 under the leadership of Trustees. The most famous object in the museum is a mechanical silver swan bought by the Bowes in 1872, which is over 200 years old and still in working order.

Bowes Museum from path

“A short, steep climb to the summit of a landmark, rocky tor with superb panoramic views”

To the south of Cleveland, beyond the flat farmland and cluttered townscape around the lower waters of the River Tees, the Cleveland Hills rise to a series of modest summits. The most prominent of these, though not the highest, is the conical Roseberry Topping, with its distinctive rocky peak.

View of Roseberry Topping from the south

Roseberry Topping

walk 19

View of Captain Cook's Monument from Roseberry Topping

Plan your walk

DISTANCE: 2 miles (3km) with possible extensions

TIME: 1½ hours

START/END: NZ570128 Newton under Roseberry

TERRAIN: Strenuous; one climb of 750ft (230m)

MAPS: OS Explorer OL 26; OS Landranger 93

Route instructions

A If the car park at the southern end of Newton under Roseberry is full there is additional parking up the road as indicated on the map. Walk from just beyond the northern end of the car park and turn right up a clear track between hedges, with fields beyond on either side. This track leads straight up to the edge of an oak wood which fringes the foot of the hill.

B Go through a gate into the wood. There are a number of paths through the trees ahead. For the easiest route turn hard left, then, after a short distance, double back to the right onto a good track which starts to climb the hill at a slant. The steep distinct stone path to the summit provides increasingly extensive views to the north and east.

1 Roseberry Topping was formed from sandstone laid down between 208 and 165 million years ago but its distinctive half-cone shape is a result of the hard sandstone cap protecting the lower layers of shales and clays from erosion. The previously conical summit changed shape in 1914 when a geological fault caused the summit to collapse though it is possible that the nearby mining of alum and ironstone was also a trigger. On a clear day the views extend to between 40 and 50 miles (60 to 80km) reaching as far as the Pennines.

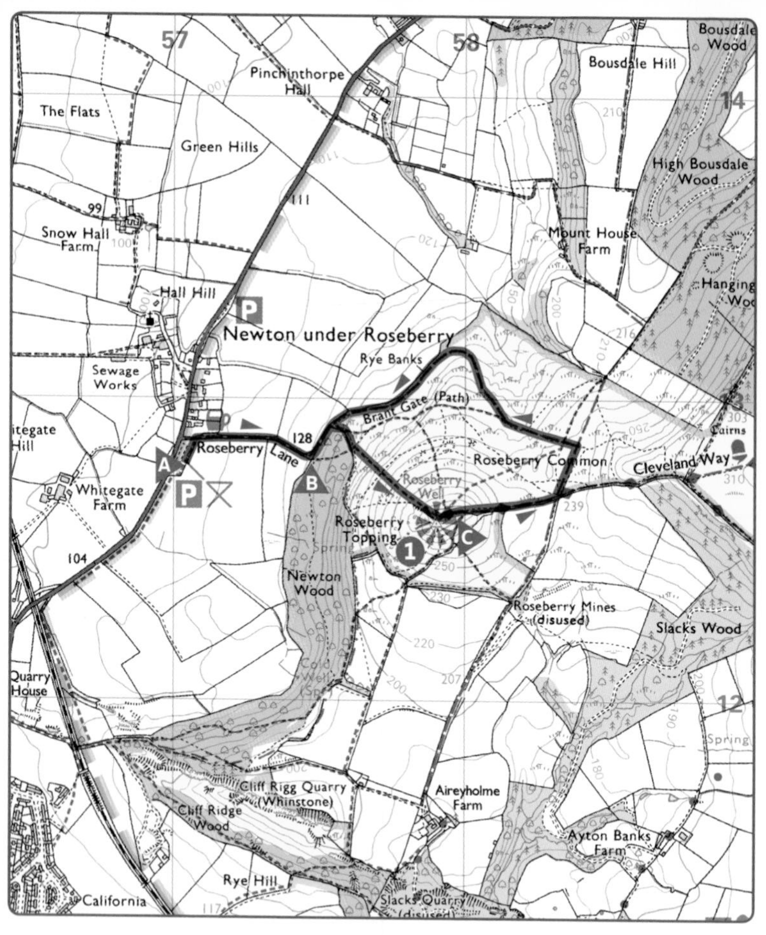

Closer features include the Cleveland Plain, the North Yorkshire Moors and the settlements along the Tees.

C From the peak there are many options. The map illustrates a possible loop to the north, but a number of other footpaths are clearly visible from the rocky summit, leading northeast to Guisborough and southwest to Great Ayton. In addition, the hill is crossed by the Cleveland Way, a long-distance footpath around the North York Moors. The Way passes Captain Cook's Monument, which is visible on a hill to the southeast. (Cook was born in 1728 at Marton, now on the southern outskirts of Middlesbrough).

Roseberry Topping

Northwest slope of Roseberry Topping

“Fine views, but not for the faint-hearted or for vertigo sufferers. A spectacular cliff-top walk, passing disused quarries along this dramatic coastline”

Boulby is a tiny coastal village near the southern border of Cleveland, on the edge of the industrial area around the mouth of the River Tees. The area is dominated by the chimneys of the huge Boulby Potash Mine, the shafts and galleries of which reach out far under the North Sea. Site of the highest cliffs in England, these slopes were once mined for alum. These mines can still be seen from the cliff-top path.

Coastline near Sandsend, south of Boulby

Boulby

Old alum quarries

Plan your walk

DISTANCE: 2–4 miles (3–6.5km)

TIME: 1–2 hours

START/END: NZ760190 Boulby

TERRAIN: Moderate; climb of 350ft (110m)

MAPS: OS Explorer OL 27; OS Landranger 94

Route instructions

A Turn left in front of a row of cottages at the western edge of the village, which sit near the edge of the 350ft (100m) cliffs – the cliffs reach a height of 600ft (180m) further to the north. A path starts beyond the cottages, along the cliff edge. This path is a section of the Cleveland Way: a long-distance footpath 112 miles (180km) in length; leading north, from Filey in Yorkshire up the coast to Saltburn, then south, to Helmsley in the Yorkshire Moors.

B Follow the path along the cliffs until it cuts left, behind the bracken covered Rockhole Hill, before rejoining the cliffs beyond. North of Rockhole Hill, the cliffs are heavily indented by the massive labours of the alum quarriers in past centuries.

C Ignore the first footpath to left, which heads across a field. A little further on, another footpath leads off between a fence and a wall, past a triangulation pillar and on to the road. Cut left to complete the shortened version of this route. Otherwise, continue beside the quarries passing an information board explaining the manner and purpose of the alum industry.

1 This area is designated a Site of Special Scientific Interest due to its fossil content being significantly different from the surrounding

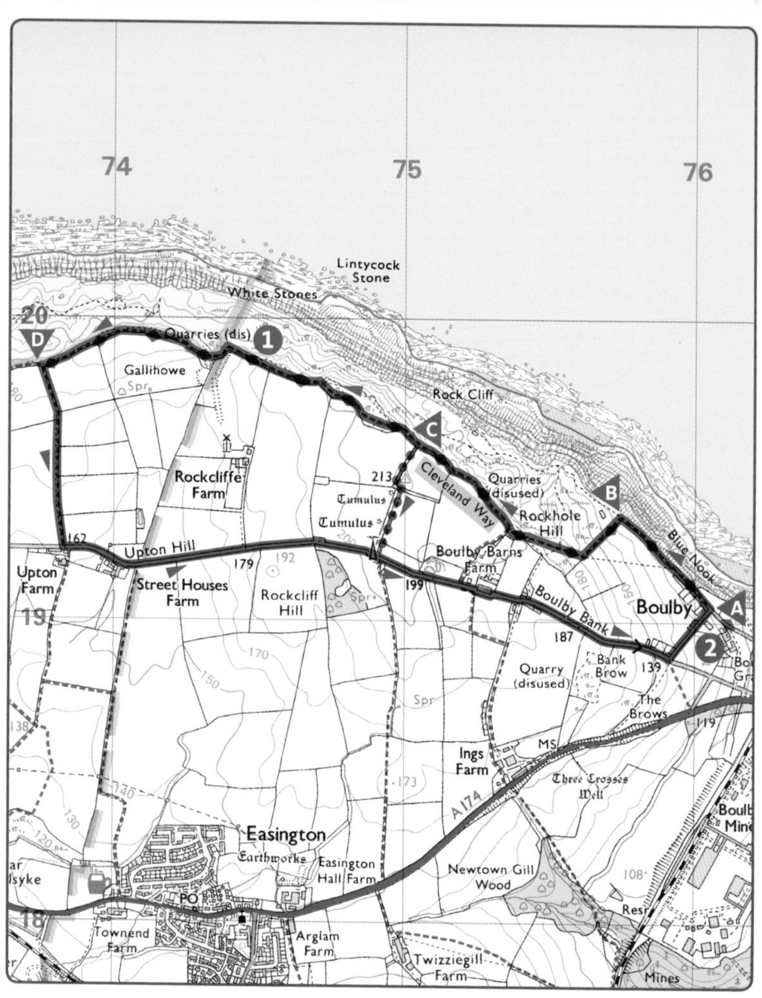

area and the discovery of several pre-historic lizards both flying and marine.

D Take the next footpath over a stile down to the left, along the left-hand side of two fields to Upton. Once the road is reached, turn left, back towards Boulby.

2 Boulby is an old Scandinavian place name meaning 'Bolli's Farm' and it appears in the Domesday Book of 1086 as 'Bolebi' or 'Bollebi'.

Boulby

View towards Teeside

Boulby Barns

Photo credits

All photographs © HarperCollins Publishers Ltd, photographer Sonia Dawkins, with the exception of:

Page 8: © HarperCollins Publishers, photographer Alex Wallace
Page 20: © Andrew Barker / Shutterstock images
Page 21: © Dominic Beddow
Page 27: © Gail Johnson / Shutterstock images
Page 28: © Dominic Beddow
Page 29: © The Chillingham Wild Cattle Association
Page 31: © Dominic Beddow
Page 36: © Gail Johnson / Shutterstock images
Page 39: © Gail Johnson / Shutterstock images
Page 48: © Dominic Beddow
Page 49: © Dominic Beddow
Page 51: © Dominic Beddow
Page 57: © Dominic Beddow
Page 65: © Dominic Beddow
Page 85: © Dominic Beddow
Page 92: © Dominic Beddow
Page 93: © Dominic Beddow
Page 95: © HarperCollins Publishers, photographer Alex Wallace

Researchers for this edition: Dominic and Patrick Beddow